Hanged at Auschwitz

T0163511

Hanged at

AN EXTRAORDINARY MEMOIR OF SURVIVAL

Auschwitz

SIM KESSEL

Cooper Square Press

First Cooper Square Press Edition 2001

This Cooper Square Press paperback edition of *Hanged at Auschwitz* (originally published in France as *Pendu à Auschwitz* in 1970) is an unabridged republication of the edition first published in New York City in 1972, with the addition of a new introduction by Walter Laqueur.

Designed by Bernard Schleifer

Published by Cooper Square Press
An Imprint of the Rowman & Littlefield Publishing Group
150 Fifth Avenue, Suite 817
New York, New York 10011

Distributed by National Book Network

Library of Congress Cataloging-in-Publication Data Available

ISBN 0-8108-1162-6 (pbk : alk. paper)

CONTENTS

INTRODUCTION TO THE COOPER SQUARE PRESS EDITION

THE TITLE IS startling—Sim Kessel *was* hanged in Auschwitz, but he was not hanged to death. Deported from France to this most infamous of all camps, he had tried to escape, but was caught and sentenced to death by hanging. But the rope broke.

Throughout his captivity he owed his survival to a number of incredible accidents (like the one mentioned above). The same is true with regard to almost everyone who lived to tell his story: some survived because they were small of stature and were overlooked during "selections," others because they were on good terms with the block leaders, the kapos, or because they could count on the solidarity of the group to which they belonged. In the case of Kessel it was the support of the boxing fraternity that saved him on two critical occasions: once it was an S.S. man with a broken nose and cauliflower ears who spared his life; on the other occasion it was a kapo who had been sent to kill him after the execution by hanging failed.

Boxing was serious business in the country of Georges Carpentier and Marcel Cerdan, and while Kessel was not champion of the world, or even of Europe, he seemed to have been better than the average amateur. He competed in some of the leading boxing rings in France, including once in the *Velo-*

drome d'Hiver, which ironically would play a tragic role in the history of the deportations of French Jews.

We learn little about Kessel's prior life from his memoir, except that he was a native of Paris, and twenty-three years of age when the Gestapo in Dijon arrested him in July 1942. The Nazis seem to have been aware of his activity in the French Resistance, but the fact that he was quite young and not in a leadership position appears to have saved him from immediate trial and execution. Instead, he endured torture for two weeks. After his interrogators had reached the conclusion that he had nothing more of interest to tell them, Kessel was shipped to Drancy, the infamous French transit camp where he was kept for nine months before being sent, in July 1943, with a transport to Auschwitz. Why was he kept so long in a transit camp? Perhaps the Gestapo had not yet caught all the members of his network, or perhaps the Nazis thought that they might still need Kessel to confront his comrades. Whatever the reason, in retrospect, the long stay in Drancy helped to save his life because it shortened his stay in Auschwitz. Hardly anyone who had arrived in Auschwitz in 1942 survived to the end of the war. The chances for those who came in 1943 were only slightly better: as Kessel writes, the average life span of a new arrival even in 1943 was merely three months, unless of course he or she was selected to join one of the categories—about three quarters of the total—destined for the gas chambers immediately after their arrival.

We would like to know more about Kessel's background, his early upbringing, his family and friends, and his politics, but his memoir is not revealing in this regard. Very few people had been active in resistance groups during the period from 1940 through 1941, when Kessel, according to his account, had first joined one. To what group did he belong? It is unlikely that he was a Gaullist, and prior to the Nazi attack on the Soviet Union the Communists were not active resistants either. Thus, it seems most likely that Kessel belonged to a left-wing Jewish group. But this vagueness is not really suspect. Once inmates had entered the hell of Auschwitz, all these things mattered little. As one survivor put it, "After a few weeks in Auschwitz we barely remembered our own first names."

Among the few names that Kessel mentions is that of his friend Henri Bulawko, who had been on the same transport from Drancy and with whom Kessel compared notes after arriving in Auschwitz. This name will not mean much to American readers, but it is quite well known in France. Bulawko had been active in the Resistance (apparently forging documents). A leading member of a left-wing Zionist group that had good connections with the Communists, he survived Auschwitz and the deadly mines of Jaworzno, and eventually became chairman of the Association of World War II Deportees, head of the Circle Bernard Lazare, and deputy head of the Roof Organization of French Jews.

When Kessel and Bulawko met in Auschwitz, they had no idea of the camp's function and purpose, and were quite optimistic about their future. But one of the veterans took them outside the barrack and pointed out two small details that they had not observed earlier: the smokestacks of the crematoria and the smell of human flesh. The idea that Auschwitz was not a concentration camp but a place for the systematic extermination of masses of people had seemed outlandish to them. They had not been entirely unaware, but they had refused to accept what seemed to be mere rumors: "This was what they had told us in France and what we'd refused to believe, and now we would be soon part of the massacre."

When Kessel arrived in Auschwitz in late July 1943, the camp had been in existence for almost two years. A small camp—mainly for prisoners-of-war and for workers engaged in construction—had been in existence even earlier on. Thus, Auschwitz was not one camp but a whole archipelago of camps, forty-five in number, with branches located near and far. Auschwitz 1 was the original site, where the German administration was located. Auschwitz 2 (Birkenau) was where the rapacious gas chambers were constructed. Auschwitz 3

(Buna-Monowitz) was mainly an industrial complex in which forced labor worked on the production of artificial rubber and of other materials important for the German war effort. The first gas chamber began operating in September 1941, but mass murder in earnest started only in April 1942. The gas chambers' killing capacity eventually reached 6,000 a day, but this figure does not include those many thousands who died from brutality, starvation, epidemics, and other diseases. The gas chambers were dismantled in November 1944; on January 27, 1945, the Red Army on its offensive entered the camp. Prior to Auschwitz's liberation, most of the surviving inmates, about 58,000, were evacuated in the Death Marches, which many did not survive. Kessel was among the lucky who did—in Mauthausen, a concentration camp located in Austria.

Auschwitz was by far the largest death camp, but it was also a camp that served a variety of other purposes. For some time, its diverse functions confused many outside observers. Usually, in Nazi Germany, there was a strict division between death camps like Auschwitz and concentration camps like Dachau and Buchenwald (most of them inside Germany), where political enemies of the Nazi regime and other suspect elements were incarcerated. The regimes in these latter camps was brutal and many inmates died or were executed, but a majority survived. (A considerable proportion of inmates was even released, some to be rearrested later.) But this refers only to political prisoners and other non-Jewish dissidents. There were, in fact, about 1,500 releases from Auschwitz, but there was not a single Jew among them.

Then there were the labor camps in which the mortality from overwork, starvation, and disease was high, but in some of them there was an even chance to survive.

Lastly, there were the extermination camps (such as Majdanek and Sobibor), which had one purpose only and from which no one returned except a handful who had been fortunate enough to escape against overwhelming odds. Auschwitz combined several of these functions and for this reason it was not immediately clear what kind of camp it was. Kessel writes that when he arrived, he had no conception of what Auschwitz was all about. But the Polish underground knew, as did the Polish government-in-exile in London and political leaders in London and Washington. It was also known in Palestine. The essential facts about the mass murder by means of gas chambers, executions, freezing to death, and starvation had been broadcast since July 1942. But many of those who had heard refused to believe.

Everyday life in Auschwitz is accurately described in Kessel's account as well as in the accounts of dozens of others. How many people were deported to Auschwitz and how many survived? For a number of reasons we shall never have exact figures. While the camp administration kept lists and prisoners were branded with a tattoo number, this does not include those immediately "selected" on the arrival ramp and sent to the gas chambers within an hour or two after his or her arrival. But in the course of meticulous investigations over almost fifty years there are now fairly reliable figures as to the total number of people deported to Auschwitz and killed there (as well as accurate numbers regarding the deportations from various countries). The total number of people deported to Auschwitz from Poland and other European countries is 1.3 million (1.1 million of whom were Jews). Hungary deported 438,000 Jews, the largest single contingent. France deported 69,000; Greece, 60,000; and the rest from a dozen other countries. Among non-Jews sent to Auschwitz the largest group was Polish (about 150,000, but there were also some 23,000 Gypsies and 15,000 Soviet prisoners-of-war). Only a few German Communists, Socialists, or other political prisoners were imprisoned in Auschwitz (most were kept in Buchenwald). There were hardly any homosexuals or religious dissenters such as Jehovah's Witnesses. Some 200,000 inmates were alive at the time the Russians liberated the camp, but it is doubtful whether even half this number survived to witness the end of the war, little more than three months later. Many perished on death marches or in other camps to which they were dispatched.

Why did some survive when others did not? The odds against surviving were high for everyone, but they were much higher for Jewish inmates than for any other category. Those lucky enough to endure managed to survive largely because of accident, as Kessel and all other former inmates have pointed out. But it is, of course, also true that those in good physical condition and those who arrived relatively late stood a better chance. It was important not to stand out, not to attract attention, and—if at all possible—to find work in a job that did not mean certain death in a matter of weeks. The will to live was a matter of crucial importance. In 1942, while Nazi Germany still seemed victorious on all fronts, it was difficult to feel optimistic about the war's outcome. But in 1944, after the major German defeats became known in the camp, the end of the war appeared within reach and survival seemed (and indeed was) a race against time. There was every inducement not to surrender but to stay alive a few more weeks or months.

Lastly, it was important to belong to a group that extended mutual help to its members. Kessel writes that he had noted from the beginning an antagonism, sometimes outright hostility, among camp inmates of various nationalities. But there was still group solidarity and not only on political lines: the group, within limits, could care for its members, extend help, even make a person disappear within the camp and survive under another identity. After his execution (which failed because of the defective rope) Kessel was officially reported dead. Yet, he survived for several weeks till the evacuation of Auschwitz under the name of another death-camp casualty.

Kessel, to repeat once again, was not a professional writer. He was not an intellectual, nor did he have literary aspirations. Had he not been a Jew living at the singular time of World War II, and a survivor of Auschwitz, he would probably never have put his recollections on paper for publication. It is precisely this artlessness—the absence of literary ambition—that helps to convey a truthful and shattering impression of what it was like to live in the hell of Auschwitz for almost two years.

WALTER LAQUEUR
June 2001
Washington, D.C.

Walter Laqueur is cochairman of the International Research Council at the Center for Strategic and International Studies, Washington, D.C., and holder of the Kissinger Chair. He has taught at Brandeis, Harvard, the University of Chicago, Johns Hopkins, and Tel Aviv University. His last academic position was that of university professor at Georgetown University. He was also director of the Institute of Contemporary History and Wiener Library, London, and is founder and coeditor of the *Journal of Contemporary History*. Among his books are *The Terrible Secret: The Suppression of the Truth about Hitler's "Final Solution"* (1980, 1998), *Breaking the Silence* (with Richard Breitman, 1986, 1996), and *The Holocaust Encyclopedia* (2001).

PREFACE

In December 1944, I was hanged at Auschwitz. The combination of circumstances that saved my life was exceptional, maybe even unique. For on the rare occasions that a rope broke or somehow got untied, the reprieve granted the condemned man was never more than a few hours: the S.S. never pardoned.

In any case, whoever wore the striped uniform of an Auschwitz prisoner was automatically doomed. To escape death was a miracle. Naturally, latecomers had the odds in their favor, provided the duration of their stay did not exceed their staying power. They were lucky to have eluded capture until the last few months of war. Those sent early to concentration camps, and who like me survived there for twenty-three months —not counting previous prison terms—were rare indeed.

Actually, the average stay at Auschwitz, and in its annex camps, was about three months. Auschwitz was not the only site of this genocide; other camps contributed to it, but none at such a rate.

Beyond this three-month period, enough to strip a man of his last reserves, survival boiled down to pure luck, the result of successive tosses of the dice. Each lucky throw granted a few days' reprieve, or at most a few weeks.

9

In this way my life was saved a hundred times, either by escaping a mortal blow or by receiving some unexpected aid. Scratched off the list of the living, we nameless men could count on none of the safeguards provided by law or the other facets of civilization.

And so to be a survivor of Auschwitz is really nothing to boast about. In that hell there was no survival of the fittest. Intelligence, courage, knowledge, vitality, the desire to live— all counted for nothing. True, there were occasions when the cleverest or the least scrupulous were able to exploit the situations they found themselves in. But common misery reduced everyone to the same level, erasing all values, breaking down all wills. Even for those in so-called soft jobs (usually obtained through pull and nearly always temporary), life or death depended on the whim of soldiers and kapos.

I have not written this chronicle of my life in a concentration camp in order to derive any personal glory from it. Were it my primary aim to appear in a good light, I would far more willingly—and more legitimately—write of my two years in the Resistance before my arrest. I can look back on this two-year stint with satisfaction, for belonging to the Resistance was enough in itself to justify a man's existence.

Why then, have I written this book, retread what is by now such familiar territory? It is true that similar rules and regulations governed life in all camps, and that what happened in one was repeated in all the others. Only the degree of torment varied.

Nonetheless it seems to me that the telling of my story will serve a valid purpose. Twenty-five years after the inmates of Auschwitz were liberated, the executioners of their dead comrades are still on trial. Only recently, some have been acquitted by the judges, and a few others let off with mild sentences. In every instance it had taken years to build up the case and to document the meticulously assembled proof of crime. There has been a general public acceptance of the S.S.'s oft-repeated excuse that they were only following orders, but every Auschwitz survivor knows that the S.S. who guarded them were guilty without exception and bore the same degree of infamy.

And so I firmly believe that my story is worth telling, if only it helps to keep the memory of these martyrs fresh. This memory is tending to fade away. A generation after the event I find there are young people who have never heard of the camps. Others have heard but simply disbelieve that they ever existed. And some assume that the horrors have been exaggerated, that it is common practice for prisoners to exaggerate their sufferings, and that, anyway, the S.S. only applied the laws of war, and that what occurred in Germany is a historical commonplace.

Such statements deeply dismay those Nazi victims who are alive to hear or read them. And yet these survivors have failed to protest. They prefer not to reopen old wounds; they would rather forget than suffer further.

Actually, there is a mixed group harder to do battle with than the merely uninformed and the skeptical. These do not deny what happened but believe in letting sleeping dogs lie. They preach silence as a policy, complain that their peace would be disturbed by any reference to the past, which forces them to inhale the stench of death. They seriously explain that it is unwise to stir up the past, which, though quite deplorable, is now definitely buried. Then there are those who are convinced that raking over old bones is morbid and out of place. Morbid, they say, because humanity gains nothing from rekindling rancor and hatred, and out of place because the Germans have truly repented the Nazi infamy.

Now, I have never confused Germany with Nazism, nor believed that the German people are criminal by nature. No race, German or other, can be condemned categorically; after all, that is what the Nazis themselves did. And from the instant that I reject the barbaric principle of wholesale collective responsibility, I am automatically prevented from attributing the crimes of the few to the many. I have known kind and humane Germans, and I have known sadistic, murderous Frenchmen. No race or nation is specifically corrupt. Only perverted individuals make an ideal of violence. That such men ruled in Germany rather than elsewhere is but one of the coincidences of history. Evil has run rampant in other places and at other times, and unfortunately there is no guarantee that it will not do so again.

To the average man of good will, it seems patently obvious that the principle of racial discrimination is scientifically absurd, and that the systematic destruction of millions of people was a monstrous crime. The fact remains that this atrocity took place in the twentieth century. Jews, Poles, Russians, and gypsies were branded as inferior and slaughtered under a belief in a hierarchy of the races. Furthermore, this insane precept had its adherents among scientists, and it was civilized men who conceived and applied the plan of deliberate, methodical extermination. Sadly, nothing allows us to assert that this ideology has disappeared, or even that it is in the process of disappearing. Quite to the contrary, Hitlerism has left an indelible mark upon the country. It still lurks in the consciousness of those it has contaminated, and much time and effort must be spent if this poison is to be eliminated.

After the war, years passed without my finding the chance or the desire to write down my memories. First of all, I had to readapt to life itself. Three years of daily ill treatment leave scars that are not only physical. Peace of mind must be slowly regained, stability reestablished, will power reawakened. For a long time, like all the others who survived, I struggled against an obsessive past. Such an obsession can become unbearable, a fact I can personally vouch for. Rest becomes impossible, slumber a series of hideous dreams. When two deportees meet, they tacitly agree not to bring up the past.

Another factor that delayed the setting down of my story was that I could only rely on memory. No one at Auschwitz was allowed to take any notes or for that matter keep paper. Writing was forbidden. And actually, even if there had been the freedom to do so, in fact one had neither the time nor the inclination. Consequently, I've had to reconstruct dates and try to be objective about events that I've lived through which at the time I hadn't the leisure to reflect on.

On the ground of truth or sincerity I could not, I think, be reproached. But on many points I wanted to be more precise. In order to do so, I spent a long time consulting with other deportees, many of whom had to be laboriously tracked down, so that they might confirm a date or an incident. It's incredible how much self-doubt one can have on happenings which are themselves incredible!

That is why I needed some help on the details. Anyone wearing the Auschwitz stripes could hardly be the ideal overall witness of everything that went on, or to take mental notes as a journalist would. At the time I was a tormented animal, blindly trying to save my own skin; and the constant necessity to steel myself against hunger, cold, illness, or beatings left me unable to ponder and reflect. Passively my brain recorded events, not trying to supply the whys and wherefores. It was all I could do just to maintain a spark of the stamina required to hold out and keep hoping. Those who lacked this vital spark sank into apathy and died through a simple abnegation of life before they had actually reached the state of physical deterioration which inevitably led to the gas chambers.

Many of these were my friends. Some of them died in my arms. And it is to them that I would like to dedicate these pages.

1 ARRESTED

I HAD JUST turned twenty-three, and my arrest was my first contact with the Gestapo.

As a Jew in France, I might have been taken in a raid or simply picked up at home. But actually it was as a member of the Resistance, returning from a mission to pick up arms, that I was apprehended.

I joined the Resistance on December 20, 1940, the result of a chance encounter with childhood friends, during my aimless wanderings around Paris. Having been demobilized a few days previously I was completely at loose ends. All I'd learned of the war was the endless monotony of a frontier post and eventually the rout.

Like hundreds of thousands of other soldiers I'd had virtually no chance to see combat. I felt this deprivation keenly. Being young, active, and adventurous I wanted to continue the fight. Not that I had any idea of the danger involved. I was aware, of course, that men of my race were being watched with particular care; the occupying power made no secret of this. But it never occurred to me to flee the peril, or even to help my family seek safety. The very moment I read the first secretly distributed leaflets and heard the first radio broadcast from London, I yearned to get in on the underground war.

I was a true child of Paris. Having grown up on the capital's sidewalks, I could not conceive of carrying on the fight anywhere else. When I was offered the chance to become part of a Resistance group, I accepted with alacrity.

For almost two years I led the dangerous life of an underground fighter. I will not go into my exploits here, not even the terrifying business which caused me to wind up in the Kommandantur on the Place de l'Opéra with a bomb in my briefcase—a bomb which never exploded. When I look back on this ambitious project I wonder if my comrades and I were not driven by some sort of madness. The execution of hostages had inspired the wild enterprise. We were rank greenhorns, new to the business, not yet fully aware of its hazards, fervently determined not to be taken for cowards, and supported by the vague and naïve hope that the enemy himself, if we were ever captured, would show a chivalrous respect for our courage.

When I was arrested on July 14, 1942, I had just crossed the demarcation line carrying a suitcase loaded with automatic pistols. These arms came from a secret stock that my battalion had buried at the time of the armistice so that they would not have to surrender them. I knew their exact location.

This was the second time I had successfully whisked across the demarcation line in both directions, the secret storage point being located south of this line at Neuville-sur-Ain. On each occasion an accomplice at the crossing point had helped me get through at night.

On the morning of the twelfth, I arrived at Chalon-sur-Saône with the intention of buying a ticket for Paris. I was trying to convey an impression of placid confidence, as if I were bringing food from the country on one of the "butter trains," but the gun-filled suitcase that I carried felt terribly heavy and my heart was beating fast. It was to beat faster.

Hardly had I received my ticket from the hand of an indifferent railway employee than a glance out the ticket window off the platform revealed a beefy German police inspector, recognizable by the badge on his chest. He was flanked on either side by two civilians, obviously Gestapo men.

There was no possibility of error. I'd had enough experience by now to know how risky the checking operations on a train could be. Since I could hardly turn on my heel without attracting the attention of the policemen, I walked onto the platform, the only thought in my head how to get rid of the damning evidence I carried.

I found the baggage-checking counter and held out my suitcase to an employee who seemed to weigh it in his hands several times, though he made no comment. I took the baggage check, put it in my pocket, and started to walk away.

I didn't dare leave the station by the same entrance I'd come in. So I went to the station bar and sat down. The sight of field-gray uniforms packing the place deprived me of the courage to seek an exit. Suddenly I was very afraid. My hands would scarcely hold my coffee cup. I began drinking coffee, or rather the roasted barley beverage that was its poor substitute.

Sitting at a nearby table was a railway worker, also drinking coffee and watching me. I can still picture his sooty face and perceptive gaze. He sized me up at once, saw that I was on the run and frantic, and also that I wasn't cool enough to conceal my driving anxiety. Outside, on the platform, an alarming scurrying had begun. Soldiers ran along the trains.

The railway man came up to me with the light of friendship in his eyes. The same intuition that had enabled him to glimpse the terror of a hunted man allowed me to understand that he would try to save me. Perhaps he would have thought twice if he'd known that I was a "terrorist." He probably assumed that I was just an innocent person trying to cross the line. In any case, without hesitation, he exposed himself to the risk of helping me pass as a worker and thus get out of the station. Almost without speaking we agreed to walk off side by side—I carrying his toolbox and wearing his cap—like two workers going home from their jobs.

"Whatever you do, don't run, we'll get out a little farther down the line."

We walked calmly along one of the tracks. Approaching a

sentinel, he anticipated my convulsive tremor and took my arm. I was certainly not over my fright.

"Stop worrying."

As it turned out, the sentinel took no notice of us. My benefactor led me through the switchyard, as far as the freight depot, then we left the depot, still together, and soon came to a quiet suburban part of town, with cozy cottages each with its own little garden. He waved at one of them a short distance away.

"I live over there. But I can't keep you at home. Whenever the Germans check the trains they also come to search the railway men's houses. Take off that way, you'll be safely in the country after about three hundred yards."

But I considered myself safe already. Naïvely reassured by the comfortable distance I had put between myself and the Germans, I shook his hand and cheerfully strode off not toward the country as my friend had advised but back to the town, thinking in my simple-minded way that I would again cross the demarcation line and go fetch another load of weapons. Not having an inkling of how thorough the police force was, I couldn't begin to estimate the danger. My awakening was rude and sudden.

On reaching the bus station I was horrified to see that departing buses were being as carefully checked as the trains. Through the window of the cafe I had so thoughtlessly entered, I could see truckloads of Germans rushing out, and policemen climbing into each bus to check travelers' papers. Again, full of trepidation, my only instinct was to get away, and fast. I was sickeningly sure that the suitcase full of guns had been discovered and that the police had a full description of me.

Whether the man at the checking counter had become suspicious of the heavy suitcase or whether he had simply given the police my description after the cache of arms had been discovered, I didn't know. Certainly, I was easy enough to recognize: blond hair, blue eyes, and the broken nose of a boxer.

I had to get out of there and I did so, avoiding all the main streets. Luck or instinct led me to that part of town near the train station which I had only left fifteen minutes previously. I hoped to appeal to the railway man who had saved me, for I didn't know another soul in Chalon-sur-Saône. I felt like a rat in a trap imprisoned in this hostile city, hopelessly lost and with all lines of exit, both trains and buses, cut off. All I could do was to keep out of sight, if possible, and wait until the intense search was relaxed.

I lay in wait for my railway man and luckily he returned home for lunch after his morning's work. I had just spent two interminable hours near his house, in a tiny garden overrun with weeds, and I was getting more nervous by the minute. My precarious shelter, risky enough before the rush hour, became ridiculous as more people left work and began to fill the streets.

At last my man took the keys from his pocket and opened his door. He had barely closed it behind him when I rang. He opened it for me.

I had decided to gamble everything—there was no alternative. The necessity for concealment overrode all other considerations. In the little dining room where my host and I sat facing each other, I poured out my entire story and told him a lot about the Resistance, trying with all my faculties to be persuasive.

He listened attentively, his clear eyes fastened on mine. I had barely finished when his wife joined us, she too coming home from work. I had to convince her as well, for my future lay in her hands. She had no objections, but simply remarked that to hide anyone was a very dangerous undertaking; the Germans had searched their house more than once.

This couple had a son in a prisoner-of-war camp, and a married daughter in Lyon. Both of them already knew about the Resistance, and regularly listened to the broadcasts from Britain.

The ordinary railway man sympathized with the underground movement and gave much secret help and support to it. In the end this couple offered me a little bedroom in their house. I spent the rest of the day there, that night, and then the following day.

At noon my host warned me that the search was still going on. All of the railway men had been interrogated and it seemed likely that all their houses would be searched. It would be best if I fled that night.

I appreciated the risks which my host ran on my account. Did I have the right to expose the lives of others to this danger?

On July 13, around ten in the evening, I stood on one of the least traveled roads leading out of the town, bidding the railway man goodbye. He had directed me there himself, making sure first that the way was clear. We shook hands. Tears were in my eyes and I believe that he was crying too. He wished me good luck and then disappeared.

I walked on into the night for several hours. A truck rumbled behind, slowly overtaking me. Its pace reassured me that it could only be a commercial truck making progress as best it could. It stopped. Its driver, whose shadowy face eludes me, had me climb in and we set off for Dijon, his destination. He didn't seem at all curious about why a young man should be hitchhiking at one o'clock in the morning. I can't remember what we talked about, not much in any case. He dropped me off on the edge of the city of Dijon just as dawn was coming up, and then drove off.

I began by seeking refuge in one of those early-morning cafes where dawn workers tend to gather. I waited there until the stores opened, then started to wander through the streets. I saw a barber opening his shutters and decided to go in for a haircut and a shave.

I can remember how deliciously safe I felt in that warm and comfortable atmosphere as the barber slapped towels on my face—the danger seemed completely passed. My natural exuberance surfacing, I chatted away happily with the barber; after these anxious days and sleepless nights it seemed I had found my way back to normal living.

Sauntering out of the shop I felt relaxed and carefree, without having any idea of what I was going to do. I realized I should get back to Paris as soon as possible, and I was just mulling over the means when I was suddenly surrounded by three men in civilian clothes.

"Your papers!"

No way of getting away from them. I must have turned white from shock. My hands shook bringing out the billfold that contained my real papers; it hadn't ever occurred to me to assume false identity.

"You're from Paris? What are you doing in Dijon?"

The man's rough accent left me in no doubt as to his nationality. Stammering, I tried to launch into some kind of explanation, but the German cut me short.

"Follow us!"

I protested, but not very convincingly. They stopped the discussion by dragging me away. I could see the butt of a pistol under the coat of one of the men. There was a car parked fifty yards away—they must have stopped when they spotted me. I balked at getting in; they had to push and shove a bit before I realized arguments were useless. The car sped off. I have no idea how long we drove or before what building we stopped —I was frantically trying to develop an alibi, some line of defense, in my head. They ordered me up a stairway, along a dark corridor, and then shoved me into a cell.

I heard the key turn in the lock. Alone in my tiny cell, I waited in bleak isolation, with neither food nor drink, throughout that day and the following night.

2 TORTURE TIME

ONLY THOSE Resistance members unlucky enough to get caught could know the awful meaning of Nazi interrogation. Certainly the Gestapo didn't invent "the question" nor did they even refine it to the nth degree. But they did develop their own style of torture. For the most part German torturers were born sadists especially chosen for that reason, or else they were trained to become so. Anyone who had dealings with the Gestapo or the S.S. soon became aware of the fact.

Enthusiastically using their fists to obtain confessions, the Nazis succeeded in their aim neither more nor less than any other police force, but they clearly brought a real zest to their work. Never did I detect among any of them the slightest hint of pity, compassion, or conscience; on the contrary, they never tired of inflicting pain or dreaming up new ways to humiliate and vilify their victims. Once their bloodied fists had broken a man's dignity and forced him to crawl and cry, they would laugh with glee. Hitler's Germany methodically trained thousands of such creatures. It is horrible to contemplate what this dehumanized army would have done unleashed in a conquered world.

Just one day after my capture they transferred me to Chalon-sur-Saône, where my crime was presumed to have taken place.

Although the Gestapo felt completely convinced that I had been the "terrorist" with a suitcase, they hadn't any real evidence. Doggedly I kept insisting that I was just a Jewish fugitive to the free zone who had come down directly from Paris to Dijon hoping to find someone to help me across. Their thorough search of me produced nothing incriminating, as I'd previously gotten rid of my ticket bought in the Chalon station, as well as the baggage check. Actually, the relatively large sums of money they found in my pockets only confirmed the story that I was trying to get away; you needed a small fortune to cross the line.

But plausible though my alibi might be, they didn't buy it. Too many things pointed in my direction, and the police were determined to make the most of my capture and force me to inform on my comrades. Since I couldn't possibly be carrying all those guns for my own personal use, I must belong to an organized group.

Thus the Gestapo's main concern was to exact the names and addresses of my colleagues from me in order to arrest them and so break up the whole network.

All of us in the Resistance were well aware of what torture could do and the danger it represented to the others when only one of us was captured. Because we had already suffered heavy losses, for some time we had been attempting to reduce contacts between us to a minimum: I knew precious few of my comrades by sight. Furthermore, it had been agreed that whenever one of us had to undertake an especially hazardous mission, the others must change their residence and identity if he did not report back after a certain period of time.

Before I left for Neuville-sur-Ain, we had decided that three days was the maximum allowable safety period. Once these three days were up, I could assume that my comrades were safely hidden.

I made up my mind to hold out for this length of time, come hell or high water, and I managed to do it. But in the bottom of my heart I can understand and forgive the unfortunates who were unable to take such punishment. During the first two weeks of my stay in Chalon-sur-Saône, I went through seven or eight interrogations. As though it were yesterday I can still remember the abominable hail of blows, kicks, and beatings with a rubber truncheon or a steel ruler. Invariably beatings were accompanied by an instructive sermon on Germany's various wartime goals and triumphs, then by shouted threats and hysterical abuse.

Perhaps it was my training as a professional boxer that gave me the ability to take torture without breaking down. In the ring a boxer learns the automatic use of reflexes—how to parry, dodge, and soften blows—and inevitably he becomes accustomed to pain. And, most important, he can only consider himself a real boxer if he stubbornly perseveres to the end, refusing against all odds to admit defeat. A few documents in my wallet had revealed my fighting career to the Nazis and I confirmed it. My profession seemed to tickle their fancy, allowing them to add a jolly sporting touch to their work.

They had the fun of pretending to be champion athletes, dishing out hooks and upper cuts with all their strength, and yet remained untouched themselves, as there was no question of allowing me to defend myself!

However, at first they didn't start roughly. Day by day they gradually and methodically stepped up the tempo of violence. At the first interrogation I was hardly touched. Its purpose was to establish my identity and determine what reasons had brought me to Dijon.

Inwardly quaking, I managed to state calmly enough that I'd been trying to cross the demarcation line to find safety in the free zone. They asked me a lot of questions about my family, my military service, and my professional occupation. Categorically I denied having the slightest acquaintance with the Resistance and declared that I had never before set foot in Chalon.

At this the cop who had brought me in gave me three fast, well-aimed slaps across the face, but the policeman asking the questions didn't insist. I thought myself lucky not to be confronted by some of the people who might have seen me at the station. Little did I imagine the Gestapo's reasoning: why waste time rounding up witnesses when a little brutality would do the trick? They just wanted a few names, after all.

Ushered back to my cell, I couldn't get much sleep despite an aching need for it. But long ago I had lost the knack of sleeping as soundly as most twenty-three-year-olds.

And early the next afternoon I had to go back to Gestapo headquarters. Now the policeman was no longer alone; he had two others with him. Together they were examining some documents in the file, and for what seemed an eternity they left me standing there before them like an invisible nervous ghost.

From time to time they would exchange a few rapid volleys of German, which I failed to grasp despite my fair knowledge of the language. The interminable wait and nerve-wracking suspense raised my anxiety to fever pitch. At long last the officer who had interrogated me before lifted his eyes to give me a piercing stare. He was a huge, beefy man with a crew cut. His French was grammatical enough but his accent so pronounced and some words so mutilated that I could only guess their meaning.

He began to speak in a rather calm voice, pointing out that as Resistance workers were not covered by the laws of warfare it was the plain duty of the German armed forces to track them down and exterminate them on the spot. Anyhow, to resist the Germans at all was stupid and pointless; no intelligent person could doubt his country's ultimate victory. As for me, he said, I was making a big mistake in denying the acts of terrorism I had committed. My lies were quite useless since he had in his possession—and here he struck the file with the flat of his hand —every proof of my guilt. Normally, he went on, I would be summarily shot, but he could spare my life if I denounced my accomplices.

In the tone of sweet reasonableness that I was to learn so well, he explained that the German Reich put great stock in the good will of French patriots—provided they would support the war effort rather than hamper it. He spoke at length.

Several times I tried to interrupt to protest my innocence, but he gloweringly insisted on silence. Amid my terrible fright I had the trivial thought that he was quite proud of the way he could handle French and wanted to show off in front of his colleagues.

I denied having done anything at all to impede the Reich's war effort. I began to repeat my alibi of the day before but they wouldn't listen; in the middle of my explanations they started chatting to one another in German as they casually strolled in my direction.

"So, you don't want to talk?"

The same question was asked several times. Then suddenly a fist crashed into my head, then another and another. As the first blows bounced off my skull, I instinctively lifted my handcuffed wrists to try to protect myself.

But the three of them alternated their attacks on me, each aiming accurately at whatever spot I'd left unguarded in my attempt to protect the last spot they'd hit. I became their plaything as they laughingly took turns pummeling me.

Not for very long, though. Because my interrogators at this first session were overenthusiastic. Only rarely would they pause momentarily to confer among themselves and then return to the same question.

"Sure you've got nothing to say?"

They hardly waited for my answer before launching another attack. Face, stomach, ribs, got their fists and toward the end, kicks from their flying boots.

They didn't take long to make a mess of my face and a pulp out of my kidneys. Unable to walk, I had to be dragged back to my cell.

Next day at about the same time, the same policeman repeated his speech in approximately the same terms, but rather perfunctorily, as if he were fairly confident that I had thought things over during the night and all he had to do now was to take down my confession.

If he assumed that the small hours of the night had weakened my resistance he was correct. It's not when you're first hit that you hurt the most. It's afterward. As the long dark hours crept by my torn body grew stiffer and stiffer. In vain I struggled to find a comfortable position; the least movement brought on stabbing pain. During that long night, in between a few brief spells of unconsciousness, my panic mounted as morning approached.

When you're in the hands of torturers you don't fear death nearly as much as the pain, which you can expect to reach unbearable intensity and which you know will culminate in mutilation and irreparable organic damage. And in addition there's always the desolate sensation of being alone and abandoned without the faintest hope of escape or rescue. Dumped onto a pallet in your lonely cell, like a wounded animal left there to die, you know you can't take any more. Wouldn't it be simpler just to give up, tell them just one name so they'll leave you alone—give the name, say, of your least important colleague? Or the one you think least of? Irresistible temptation backed up by solid argument fed with inevitable self-pity when with brimming eyes you consider the cruel sacrifice you've already made. Your tattered face, your torn and still bleeding eyebrows, etc.

Under torture the moral resistance of even the strongest character dwindles when that person has a moment to dwell on his former life: his home, wife, mother, friends—and the alluring prospect of regaining it all if he'll only talk. Yes, my torturers might well have succeeded in getting a confession out of me had they been clever enough to come back at night, to capitalize on those periods of deep despair when I wept bitterly over my own plight.

For by the time morning came I had recuperated. Standing once more defenseless before the enemy, I seemed to have found new courage. Despite my terror some measure of pride had come back so that now my conscience revolted at the thought of betraying a single comrade. As the crop-haired German began his speech once again, I grated my teeth and whispered to myself, "I won't talk, I won't!"

At such a moment it's vital to summon up those whose fate depends upon you, to remember the everlasting remorse that would follow a moment's weakness and the shame you would have to bear for the rest of your life.

The avalanche of blows fell as before, but this time lasted longer. To work themselves up to a frenzy the three men as they struck me bellowed obscenities at the top of their lungs. They shouted in both languages, of which the German insults were far the fouler and more obscene. Not that I paid much attention to the verbal onslaught, for soon I was howling loudly myself. I tried to ward off the blows as best I could, but that was no use and I could feel my will power stretched to the breaking point. Through a mist of agony I felt myself giving up.

Now they decided to change tactics in order to give their bruised fists a rest. Taking up steel rulers they started to whip me on my bare behind, after first bending me at right angles over a table and lowering my trousers. Each blow was accompanied by some unprintable epithet: after a while each hit took off a strip of flesh. I screamed myself hoarse before mercifully passing out. Next thing I knew I was being dragged out of the room, drenched from the water that had partly brought me back to my senses.

In all, I was tortured over a two-week period. At the next session, and from then on, there were about half a dozen thugs working on me—huge brutes who bounced my body from one to the other as if playing football, at the same time laughing a good deal and egging each other on. Somewhere about this time, thank God, my capacity to feel pain began to recede a bit.

Perhaps in order to revive my dulled senses, at the last session they started pushing match sticks under my fingernails and slashing me lightly with a knife, just enough to break the skin and let the blood pour out. They worked on my bare torso, carefully seeking the most sensitive areas. Every other minute they'd warn that they were about to finish me off with a dagger or have me shot if I persisted in silence. *"Kaput, kaput!"* In their eyes, anyone challenged by mighty Germany was kaput—be he French, Russian, English, American, or Jew.

For a long time they had refused to believe I was Jewish, probably because of my physical appearance, which, ironically, closely approximated the blond Aryan ideal favored by the Nazi ideologists. But finally they had to accept my racial origins.

Today when I try to analyze their reactions I have to admit that, paradoxical as it may seem, the fact that I was a Jew saved my life. The Nazis soon grew bored with my simple case—an ordinary fugitive trying to escape into the free zone. If they hadn't lost interest, I might well have been tortured to death. Naturally they had more serious problems to solve, more important prisoners to interrogate. I know that the prison was full of them.

When I left the room for the last time, dragged or carried by two policemen, I thought I was dying and didn't care. I was half conscious, soaked to the skin, and covered with blood. From the depths of my misery came flashes of joy and a grim satisfaction: "I got the better of them. They've killed me, but I got the better of them." Rather like a boxer at the end of a grueling fight—battered but victorious. My physical condition, however, was one that a boxer would never attain in the ring. My purple face was a mass of raw wounds, my eyes swollen shut, my body a tattoo of angry cuts and infections. That steel ruler in addition to shredding my behind so that I couldn't sit had also caused my testicles to swell. Now they were blue, enormous and atrociously sensitive.

Such was my peculiar state of mind and body when the torture sessions finally ended at last. It had been hell, but I'd lived through it and without giving the enemy so much as a nugget of information. In the long run, I had even almost adjusted to torture; the blows no longer hurt so much, perhaps from sheer nervous exhaustion as well as numbness. Toward the end, all I could feel at each blow was a sort of faraway shock, as though someone else were being hit. By then I was floating in such a comatose state that not even the most diligent torturer could snap me out of it.

From the moment I realized that the torment had really stopped I began to slowly come back to life. A young healthy body has remarkable recuperative powers, particularly as at that time I still had all of youth's carefree exuberance and optimism. I congratulated myself on my luck—holding out and getting away with it! It seemed more and more probable that the Gestapo had pigeonholed my file, postponed any definitive decision to some other time. Undoubtedly they had more pressing business at hand. My hope that they'd dropped my case for the time being became a joyful certainty when I was transferred to the jail at Dijon.

Compared to the Gestapo's foul dungeons, my new cell seemed positively luxurious. It had the average comfort of a French prison with a straw mattress and adequate facilities. For two weeks now I'd hardly eaten and never washed. My uncared-for gashes were festering under my torn and filthy underwear and the same suit I'd left Paris in. Walking was so painful that I dragged along bent double, still wincing at every step.

Upon my arrival at the prison I was pleasantly surprised to discover that a human being could wear a German uniform; he was an old soldier drawn from the reserves, newly arrived in France to act as turnkey in the prison. I say "old," but he was probably about forty-five. And my arrival gave him his first glimpse of what the Schlag did to members of the Resistance. Maybe one day he would become hardened to grisly sights, but he was genuinely horrified by my mutilated body and face, the clots of dried blood stuck onto my clothes. During my stay in Dijon—slightly over two months—this man was not only friendly but helpful.

Finding that I spoke a little German, he immediately took an interest in me. I believe too his kindliness may have stemmed from his paternal instinct—he had a son on the Russian front. At this time the Wehrmacht was suffering severe losses on the eastern front, with one crippling defeat after another. It was also the time of El Alamein and Rommel's retreat across Africa.

We prisoners were well aware of the war's progress: our group of secret militants followed the march of events with passionate interest and got our information from the horse's mouth. Even before I'd taken off on my fatal trip into the free zone, the tide seemed to have turned against the Germans, for obviously their military might alone could not cope with their vast expansion. Their only allies were the Italians, who were unable to help them in Africa and were even responsible for the Axis's first defeats. Finally, the failure before Moscow shattered once and for all the myth of the Wehrmacht's invincibility. The whole world then knew that the concept of a lightning war was a thing of the past, that the Resistance was gaining strength day by day, and that the German army would be forced into a long battle in which it would inevitably perish because of the immense forces gathered against it.

I never doubted the final outcome, and this confidence reinforced my power to resist. The kind German veteran who showed such compassion for me obviously wasn't one of Hitler's most fervent admirers. Nor was he actively against Hitler. There were many Germans like him—World War I veterans not young enough to be swayed by propaganda and regimentation, yet not committed enough to any ideology, whether pacifist or Marxist, to be positively anti-Nazi.

My guard's wary mentality was more or less that of all Germans who waited to see what Hitler would produce. Yet whether applauding his successes or criticizing his failures, they were ready at the drop of a hat to obey and patriotically serve their country. More than once my guard let me know that he did not expect the Germans to win. Furthermore, he said philosophically, having gone through defeat previously he knew there were a lot worse things in life than that.

I have forgotten this soldier's name, but I would like to

see him today to express my gratitude. At nightfall he would come to my cell and produce from his pocket whatever he'd been able to find in the way of food, generally something from his own meal.

From the first day he took me under his wing. Obviously ignorant of Nazi interrogation methods, he was naïvely indignant that they had not thought to take me to the infirmary. At once he found what was needed to make bandages and at nightfall undressed me to clean my pus-filled wounds. I can remember how he used to feel my pulse or put his hand on my forehead to check whether or not I had a fever. I am sure that he lacked any kind of medical training, yet I could have been nursed no better by the most skilled physician.

Perhaps it was his good will as much as his actual ministrations that led to my quick recovery. Within only ten days or so there remained only traces of the nightmare I'd gone through. My face was almost back to normal and healing scabs had begun to form over my cuts. Adequate food, thanks to the extras the guard brought, helped my convalescence. Thus the fare, though of mediocre quality, was relatively abundant and I quickly regained my normal weight.

Yet my ordeal had left a strange aftermath I couldn't seem to get rid of. Sometimes my reasoning powers simply left me. In the middle of a conversation with my benevolent guard I would suddenly be seized with a terrible fear that made me tremble and shake. In my hallucinatory state I felt sure that the door would suddenly be flung open and in would troop my torturers. I could almost hear them bellowing what they were going to do to me. And no matter how I tried to get hold of myself, pure terror would overwhelm me so that my teeth chattered violently and sweat poured from me. And then my guard, seeing my condition, would attempt to reassure me, saying that the war couldn't last much longer and soon we'd both be back home. But sometimes he would just gaze at me sympathetically for a long time, then sigh and go away.

Although he spoke only German, we were soon able to understand each other very well thanks to what I already knew of the language and what I picked up through talking with him. He described a lengthy World War I campaign he'd fought in on the French front, where he'd been wounded and hospitalized. Proudly he showed me pictures of his wife, his son on the Russian front, and his two young daughters. Of course there was a whole world of difference between him and me. Not only were we of different nationalities but we also differed in race, age, and temperament. He was just as calm and disciplined as I was impatient. Nonetheless there was a curious bond of friendship between us which never wavered for a moment. Maybe, on his part, it all sprang from his indignation at seeing my maimed body. He could not comprehend how a person could attack a helpless man. When he learned how they had driven matches under my nails and worked over my skin with the point of a knife, he couldn't conceal his anger. Real Germans, he said, could never perpetrate such atrocities, which stained the honorable reputation of their country in the eyes of foreigners. He never thought to ask what I had done to deserve such treatment. But when I told him I was Jewish his liking for me didn't seem dampened in the least; to the very end he remained friendly, helpful, and sincere.

During my prison stint in Dijon I was able to get together with other Frenchmen who had been locked up for various reasons. My own cellmate, already there when I arrived, was named Weiss. Having fled from Alsace and been arrested as he crossed the demarcation line, he was later—forcibly— drafted into the German army. Subsequently sent to the Russian front, he got himself killed—literally. Several years later when I visited his family they told me that his death had been a deliberate sacrifice on his part: he had simply put himself in the path of bullets so that he would not have to fight for the Germans.

Four days after my arrival, we were joined by Vinaucourt, who had also been arrested as he tried to cross the line to rejoin the F.F.L. (French Forces of Liberation). I got to know him during the brief evening exercise. Walking single file in the prison courtyard we just by chance passed one another. Later I was to encounter him again in the striped uniform of a concentration camp inmate at Jaworzno.

I was allowed to write home, though my letters naturally went through the hands of the censor, who tried to glean a little information from them. They did, however, reach their destination. My parents also wrote me and sent along some parcels that boosted my morale. From several allusions slipped into their letters I knew they had already warned the network.

At my arrest they had taken away practically everything I had on me, including over ten thousand francs, my total assets. Half of this sum was hidden in my glasses case. The sergeant searching me opened the case, grabbed the money, and slapped me. Now, to my utter astonishment, the money was scrupulously handed over to me intact as I left. It turned out to be extremely useful on the train back to Paris at the end of my three-month detention.

3 DRANCY

Toward the end of October a uniformed secretary, holding a sheaf of rubber-stamped documents, opened the door of my cell to announce in bad French that as I was being transferred the following day I should now prepare for my departure.

"*Nach Paris,*" he said and left, again without further explanation.

I seethed with excitement, wondering if this news meant freedom, but I knew better than to give way to any optimism. I turned the news over in my head testing every possibility. The range was enormous, of course—anywhere from permanent liberty to being sent up before a firing squad.

I spoke to my cellmate about it, but he knew no more than I did. Now he was faced once more with the prospect of being alone. Close friendships are made very quickly in prison.

That evening my friendly keeper came in with a carefully tied package for me. He had heard the news and he had brought a snack for me to have on the journey next day. Apparently the case had gone before the courts that ruled on such matters. I was condemned to be deported but, being Jewish, I would first be interned at Drancy, where special trains were made up.

German logic worked that way. Since they had been unable to obtain a confession they lacked any proof of my underground activities. Yet on the sheer ground of my Jewishness they could still condemn me to slow death! Still, though the end result might be the same, at least I got a postponement.

Because of course any delay helped. To a strong, optimistic youth, not being killed immediately opened up a whole new vista of possibilities—German collapse, American invasion, or my escape from prison. Little did I dream then how tenderly I would have to nourish those hopes or how despite the best of care they would die and then have to be resurrected again.

It was sad saying goodbye to my only German friend. He tried to cheer me up, again predicting a quick end to the war and an imminent homecoming. But we both wept as we shook hands. Then he turned away and closed the iron door behind him. I never saw him again.

Early the next morning two French cops appeared and snapped some handcuffs on my wrists. I was surprised by their nationality, having expected German uniforms. I had forgotten that there was such a thing as collaboration, when in fact it was the norm in prison circles.

These two seemed average specimens of their ilk. They performed their job efficiently, following their written instructions with care in order to avoid all complications. "An order to take the person of Sim Kessel, held in the civil prison of Dijon (Côte d'Or) and escort him to the camp at Drancy (Seine) by railway, handcuffed." They knew from experience all the reactions they might run into—sudden bolt to a window, a show of determined resistance, emotional collapse, or piercing screams to attract a crowd. They seemed to diagnose me as one of those crazy kids who might do something reckless, and gently but firmly warned me not to cause them any trouble.

"We've had enough of that kind of stuff!"

I wasn't about to give them any trouble. But one longing had been spinning through my brain since the previous night —before being dragged into an unknown future I wanted to get a glimpse of someone dear to me. I adored my parents,

especially my mother whom I hadn't seen for almost three
months. Seeing that the cops were French gave me encouragement, and I thought perhaps they might allow me to see my
parents a few minutes to say goodbye. Surely a Frenchman
wouldn't have the heart to refuse me that? Because in the first
place, who would know about it? Once in Paris it would be
so simple to go directly from the train via the métro to the
Place Daumesnil. It would only take a moment and it wasn't
much to ask. Even a condemned man was allowed one last
cigarette!

In the compartment where we finally settled after waiting
hours on the platform, I threw out a few opening gambits in
the form of stupid little questions; nothing is more natural than
to chat with one's guards, and no rule says they must remain
mute. The sergeant was on my left, I was handcuffed to his
companion on my right. I couldn't move my right arm without
moving his left arm along with it and making a metallic clatter
in the process. We used our free hands to smoke.

Gradually my innocuous remarks seemed to unthaw the two
slightly. But they remained vigilant. Even when I asked permission to go to the toilet, there was no thought of letting me
go freely. My Siamese twin freed his own wrist only to put the
handcuff on my other hand so that now my two wrists were
together. I could unbutton my fly but that was about all. How
could I get away, handcuffed? But anyway the policeman accompanied me to the men's room and held the door open, all
the while watching me with a beady eye.

Returning to the compartment, we started talking about the
war, the Russian front, the African front, rumors of a landing.
On every point the policemen remained completely neutral,
choosing their words with care. Oddly, they seemed quite ignorant of Rommel's defeat at El Alamein and his flight toward
Tunisia.

"How do you know . . . ?"

Thin ice! Hastily I switched to their families. Families always strike a chord. When they cozily produced photos of their

children I countered with a snapshot of my parents and then put my case to them: that once at the Gare de Lyon we make a little detour to the Place Daumesnil, only a stone's throw away. How easy it would be! And the same taxi that whisked us to the Place Daumesnil could, a few moments later, serve to take us to the northern suburbs. I would pay for the taxi, naturally . . . just ten minutes to kiss my parents goodbye.

At that the policemen's whole demeanor changed: cordiality vanished and they stared at me icily as if offended. In the lengthy silence that followed, my request began to appear presumptuous, then exorbitant, scandalous, exceeding the bounds of decency, a serious offense against morality. At last the sergeant yawned and said that of course they could do no such thing.

Then, relenting, he added that it would mean their jobs. Normally they'd allow a prisoner to say goodbye to his family, they were human themselves. But with the German occupation . . . and anyway, they didn't know what crime I'd committed.

It sounded all too plausible. Of course they couldn't become accomplices to someone who might have been a real criminal. The fact was, they didn't even ask me about my activities, and I was hardly in a position to supply any information. I sank back defeated, blinking back tears of disappointment.

But a moment later, after we had shared our snacks and a bottle of red wine, they themselves resumed the subject. They said that they would like to help me out, but there was nothing in it for them. Or words to that effect. I immediately understood. I drew out my bulging wallet and this time the matter was easily settled: agreed, on the basis of my ten thousand francs!

At that time this sum would have paid a policeman's wages for six months. And it amounted to my entire assets, within a few centimes. I had converted my worldly assets into liquid cash in case of emergency—if I'd had to pay a smuggler to replace a Resistance member at the frontier failing me for some reason.

Now it turned out that these policemen demanded that much money—all of it, and they drove a hard bargain. I first offered them five thousand francs but they demanded twice that amount.

Now the smugglers for whom this money had been earmarked *did* run risks. In addition to the risk of being betrayed, they had to avoid machine gun nests hidden in hedges, patrols which constantly changed schedules, and packs of hounds set on them when they were suspected.

But these policemen!

Not that I thought anything of it at the time; in fact I even felt vaguely grateful, due to their granting-a-favor attitude. But for years to come, during bouts of insomnia in the wee small hours, I had plenty of time to ponder the moral code of those two men.

After all, what did they risk? At worst, even if they had let me slip away, pretending I'd escaped—and genuine escapes had occurred more than once—they wouldn't have gotten into very much trouble. But I wasn't even asking that. All I asked was to say goodbye to my parents, and for granting me that privilege, and with the full realization of the horror that they were leading me to afterward, they just cold-bloodedly fleeced me.

All in all, the men of the Gestapo were perhaps less base; at least they had the excuse of having been brainwashed by the Nazi ideology.

So there I was late that afternoon in the crowded train station, a handcuffed prisoner arousing the other passengers' mild curiosity. Only mild, for they had already seen plenty. They had acquired the habit of not asking questions on such occasions, and even walking on a little faster. One never knew. It was so easy to get caught in a roundup because you happened to be there, an innocent bystander. Fear was visible everywhere, it could be seen on the faces of people hurrying along the sidewalks, on the faces of people waiting in the lines. Fear permeated everyone—members of the Resistance, collaborators, those on neither side. Nobody felt secure any more, no one could count on anyone else. We who resisted the occupation desperately feared getting caught; those who collaborated worried about the future. Those who had no ax to grind at either camp knew that their neutrality couldn't last and they dreaded having to make a choice.

So the milling Paris throngs seemed to me, that October afternoon in 1942, a crowd poisoned by anxiety, stress, and deprivation. It occurred to me that this might be my last glimpse of Paris.

We took the underground and got off after only three stops. Here were the streets I'd grown up in. And here again I am ashamed to say I bribed my two keepers. I asked them to re-move my handcuffs so I'd be spared the embarrassment of walking manacled past the neighborhood shops where I was known. I had to dicker with them; at first they pretended they wouldn't consider such a thing. And so I promised them five packages of cigarettes I had hidden at home. No, five packages each, insisted the policemen. And I accepted their demands.

Those ten minutes at my parents' went by very quickly, yet I wasn't tempted to try to outstay the allotted time. It was too awful, seeing my mother cry.

I came back with a light suitcase and joined the two police-men waiting for me on the landing. We walked down the seven stories and set off in a taxi across Paris.

Toward Drancy.

I stayed nine months in the camp there. Thousands upon thousands of Nazi victims passed through this detention camp, where they were imprisoned before being sent on to Auschwitz.

Drancy, this vast penal institution just outside Paris, had no other purpose than to temporarily absorb the flow of the condemned and to prevent traffic jams at Auschwitz and Mauthausen, whose gas chambers and ovens couldn't keep up the pace, however fast new ones were built. It was impossible to kill everyone at once.

Anyway, every ounce of work had to be drawn from the victims, at whatever price, before they were murdered. The Nazi program called for the slaughter of millions—children, old people, and all ages in between, of both sexes. Most of the relatively few survivors of Nazi persecution owe their lives to the simple fact that the German murder factories were overloaded. They simply had too much human flesh to liquidate, and therefore had to postpone some arrests until later, to avoid clogging the killing machines.

And so, along with other camps in France, Drancy was an antechamber to death. The French authorities, or what remained of them, didn't just accede to the policy of official mass murder, but obligingly lent a helping hand. Members of the French police force guarded the doomed, and these policemen succeeded in making a tidy profit from their jobs.

They played a large part in the gigantic enterprise of pillaging Jewish assets, most of which went to Germany, where a few scraps found their way into private German hands. Some crumbs remained for French turncoats.

For in this vast ant heap of condemned flesh there was no human desire, however trifling and easy to gratify, that did not line some policeman's pocket. There was a standard rate for delivering a secret letter and for bringing back a reply. And there were small comforts with which one tried to mitigate one's fate while awaiting deportation to Germany. One paid for these comforts from the contents of a suitcase hastily filled before being arrested. Thus an incredible traffic in jewelry, watches, furs, and articles of clothing had turned the entire camp into a gigantic bartering market. Tobacco and coffee were the basic currency.

Among this wretched mass of humanity, twenty jammed into a room, were individuals from every social level—millionaire bankers to penniless bums. All of them knew that, barring a miraculous change in the war situation, eventually and inevitably they were going to find themselves naked together awaiting death. At that moment they would be on perfectly equal terms. One might have thought that they would pool their resources, at least within the realm of possibility, to try to form a united front against their common misfortune. This never happened, or practically never. A few sensible people tried to preach wisdom, but they were preaching in the desert. The will to survive is stronger than reason. It continues against all odds, matching its determination against the bleakness of the situation. Later on in the extermination camps I saw men still fighting over a bread crust as they were being herded to their death. At Drancy, prisoners quarreled over everything—some man wanted a girl and refused to share her with anyone else, or someone might feel cheated over a hand of poker or bridge. Simultaneously the camp was a market, a den of thieves, and a bawdy house. Among the inmates murder was not uncommon.

That famous racial solidarity so denounced by Nazi theoreticians as a peril to the world proved to be pure legend. It was every man for himself. Even in a camp like Auschwitz, where the deportees were mostly Jewish, they never seriously attempted to organize themselves into a solid bloc of opposition to their enemy. Such loose-knit groups as they did form were by nationalities, which of course included non-Jews. National origins and common culture made people feel closer than did any racial or religious ties.

The prisoners at Drancy lived according to the eternal law of the jungle. Some bought their freedom with gold, through strange deals involving both German officers and French policemen. Loopholes could always be found in the great ideological doctrine of racial purity—provided the price was right.

Degradation and demoralization showed itself in many ways, one being a sexual promiscuity that rose to amazing proportions. Fear of imminent death drove the prisoners to a frenzy of wild excesses, sweeping aside all shame and moral values. Women gave themselves to all comers, occasionally to obtain a favor, mostly in an attempt to forget what awaited them, to squeeze a little pleasure out of life before they left it. Some practiced open prostitution out of frank perversity.

In this hell I met a few old acquaintances and made some new ones. Naturally I gravitated to those who had like me played a part in the Resistance. We tried vainly to create some sense of organization out of chaos, but there were just too many people. Because we could only work within a restricted area, our influence too was limited. Furthermore, our original group kept diminishing as contingents left the camp, so that we would have to recruit newcomers and start all over again. From time to time one of our friends would receive the dread summons; he would gather up his pathetic belongings and climb into a truck. I never again saw any of those who left.

But at times we had reason to hope. News would filter in that even the barbed wire couldn't keep out. One of our main pastimes consisted of patiently gathering up and weaving together bits and pieces of information which reached us and endlessly discussing their significance. At that time Germany was losing on every front. Having suffered defeat at El Alamein, the Afrika Korps had completely lost the initiative and was forced to take a defensive position on the Marth line. On November 8 hope rose again when we heard of the Anglo-American landing in North Africa, though at the same time it was by way of being a disappointment—a disappointment because what we really wanted was an invasion of France, and operations in Africa only intensified the political backbiting we didn't understand. Our comrades in the Resistance seemed to have been bypassed by the events. But almost simultaneously the glad tidings reached our ears that the Germans had been stopped at Stalingrad. This defeat, whose importance was minimized by the subservient press and radio, appeared to us as an event of major importance, and this in the long run proved to be true. We knew that Germany was being badly bombed and, naturally enough, we tended to overestimate the capabilities of the Allied forces. We predicted the enemy's imminent collapse. Yet history had decided that peace was far off.

By the time my number was up at Drancy, I had become what in that place was a real old-timer. Despite the shifting composition of the camp personnel I had somehow stuck there longer than most, and had my own network of friends and contacts.

Many times we had toyed with the idea of escape, but we never found the means. Shortly before my arrival at the camp, a group of militants had dug a tunnel and a few of them had even escaped. But of course this success only rekindled our keepers' vigilance; it was impossible for us to attempt the same thing again. Everyone realized the awful consequences of a failure, and even a successful escape would mean terrible reprisals on any prisoner's family who couldn't find sanctuary. This was my situation.

Hearing my own name called came as no surprise; I'd been expecting it. Moreover, being summoned came almost as a relief despite grim forebodings of where I was going. The stifling atmosphere of Drancy had become unbearable. I was not tortured there or even ill treated. I had almost enough to eat and was not forced to work. But I was surrounded by these pitiful dregs of humanity, men, women, and children ravaged by fear. Especially the children. Some nights I still dream of the children at Drancy, clutching at their mothers' skirts and crying incessantly.

4 TO THE END OF THE NIGHT

WE human cattle about to be transported stumbled through the barbed wire surrounding Drancy. There were nearly fifteen hundred of us—men, women, and children mixed together. Enough to make up a trainload.

We represented all ages, classes, and physical conditions. Some wore well-tailored topcoats and carried expensive leather suitcases, others were bent and careworn, with bundles slung over their shoulders. Many women carried children and were already on the verge of collapse from strain and weariness. There were Jews, gentiles, Resistance fighters, and peace-at-any-pricers, there were the violent and the meek. Some had been in the Resistance but got caught as a result of being denounced. Others had been picked up as they fled over the demarcation line or tried to cross a frontier. Some had been grabbed from the streets during mass roundups, and some plucked from their beds. And there were some who knew absolutely nothing, had done nothing, weren't Jewish, and had no idea why they were there. They had been arrested at home just as they were getting dressed to go to work. They wore themselves out protesting, but their pleas might as well have been hurled at a stone wall, and some were beaten. At last they had given up hoping that efficient German administration and the highly touted German sense of organization would reveal the monstrous errors of mistaken identity and set them free. Eventually they would perish ignominiously like the others in the hell of the camps. Meanwhile they wore around their necks placards proclaiming them "Friend of the Jews."

It was July 18, 1943. The French police turned us over to the soldiers of the Wehrmacht. We were herded into buses and then driven to the station. It was entirely a matter of chance as to whom you were with in the buses. My few friends were scattered in the throng and I soon lost sight of them completely. I did my best to help and comfort the women laden down with their children and baggage and already shivering from fear. They were all strangers to me, my fellow passengers on the crowded Paris bus they used to transport us.

Most passengers huddled in a corner, darkly silent, concentrating on trying to hold on to the few meager possessions they had carried with them, their last tangible assets. A few always felt the need to talk; there was one in particular sounding off, a typical unstoppable Parisian monologist with a braying accent, pompous tone, and know-it-all manner which implied that all mysteries could be dissolved and the future seen crystal-clear if you would only listen to him. "What are they going to do with us? It's simple. Workers. Germany needs workers. The Russian front has swallowed all their manpower reserves. We'll be replacing workers in the armament factories and believe me, a worker making a shell is just as useful as any soldier. They'll have to feed us well, of course, for the sake of productivity."

It was almost as if this idiot had concluded that, all things considered, we should be offering up prayers of thanksgiving. Yet we listened to him and tried to believe the notion that we despised ones could live under acceptable conditions while good Germans were being killed at the front. Inside, of course, each of us nourished his own despair. We had heard rumors of concentration camps for years now, ever since Hitler had become Chancellor of Germany in 1933, ten years previously.

The thought of escape consumed me. If only I'd been closer to the exit, I could have tried to jump from the rolling bus. But we were all packed in like sardines. I could never have acted quickly enough to escape the two armed Germans watching us.

Before long we stood in silent groups outside the station, which one I do not know, until our captors herded us onto the platform. Soldiers, soldiers, everywhere we looked. The instinctive aversion a Frenchman feels at the sight of foreign uniforms was multiplied a thousandfold. What was to become of us now?

A strong detachment of S.S. troops surrounded the area where our train was being made up. And in rattled those gloomy wooden wagon trains with signs on them saying "Men: 40. Horses lengthwise: 8."

Onto these trains we were piled, not just forty but eighty and more—men, women, and children indiscriminately lumped together. A classification would be made when we reached our destination. Soldiers rounded us up en masse toward the freight car's open door, and after that there was no longer any question of being polite or helping the weaker. It was every man for himself.

The soldiers were shoving us aboard efficiently but not too brutally because we were still in Paris, where they had to keep up a pretense of civilized behavior. As they pushed they shouted "Schnell, schnell!" Within a couple of minutes the car was jam-packed. We didn't even have time to look at one another before the doors clanged shut, hermetically sealed.

Darkness fell, we were in pitch blackness, but soon our eyes grew accustomed to it and we could distinguish the slits through which a ray of light could pass, along with a tiny breath of air. We tried to get comfortable as best we could, for it was to be a long trip, but it was not easy to untangle our legs from our neighbors and find a spot to set down our bags. Space suddenly became a precious luxury, something everyone desperately craved. We had to plan for the oncoming night, arrange for a tiny piece of floor where we could try to stretch out perhaps or at least sit down. For a while there were a few valiant pleasantries among the captives squashed in a wooden cage, but they soon fell flat, and our silence was disturbed only by the whimpering of frightened children.

The train started off slowly. Exhaustion overwhelmed the mass of bodies stacked against each other, a grinding exhaustion intensified with each jolt. We began by excusing ourselves for bothering our neighbors. But who wasn't bothered? And soon we stopped being polite. The more our backs or our legs or our bottoms hurt, the more we tried to surreptitiously grab a little more space. We pushed against our neighbors and were pushed by our neighbors in turn. The temperature started to rise, as the freight car was enclosed and body heat had no outlet. And so we started to take off our coats, being absurdly careful not to wrinkle them.

It was not long before we became thirsty, and the hopeful ones still labored under the belief that we would be given food and water. Apparently they had failed to grasp at all what was happening. Some had brought bottles of water with them, but these were empty in no time and then they were put to another use. The only place to urinate was through a slot in the skylight, though whoever tried this usually missed, spilling urine on the floor and making the others complain. Soon complaints turned into insults and curses. Under the grip of fear and misery, we do not for long retain our thin veneer of civilization.

Night came. We wanted sleep and we did despite our wretchedness, but what sleep! When dawn finally rose and filtered through the skylight's grid we were all quite ill and shattered, crushed not only by the weight of fatigue but by the stifling, moist atmosphere and the foul odor of excrement. Adults as well as children had relieved themselves during the night. There was no latrine, no provision. Before leaving, the soldiers had named a chief, someone to maintain order inside the car, and this individual seemed rather proud of his position, though actually it consisted mainly of latrine duty. Since there was no latrine, he had produced as a substitute a large metal can that had formerly contained food. Emptying it created a terrible problem. On top of everything else, a lot of people had vomited on the floor. We were to live for days on end breathing these foul smells, and soon we lived in the foulness itself.

During the first night someone had the bright idea of testing the floor where he was lying, near the middle of the car. For hours and hours he scraped at the wood with his penknife to open a crack. Eventually the floor gave way a bit, and when dawn came he called me. He was just a youngster, a boy of about seventeen, bold and adventurous. I crawled over the stretched-out bodies to where he was working and considered our chances of escape. They seemed fair enough. With a few good men and whatever we could find in the way of tools, we could pry open a hole in a very few minutes. Although the floor was thick the half-rotted wood could easily be worn away. It was not yet daylight. We might, I thought, make the most of the next stop. Dangerous, certainly, but when it's a matter of now or never you have no choice.

A few of us united our efforts and stamped on the floorboard until it cracked. Success seemed in sight when suddenly we began to hear mutters of protest behind us, mutters that gradually swelled to a veritable chorus. First some of the men complained, then their wives stridently took up the argument. Yes, they said, some might get loose to make it. The ones left behind would have to take the rap for the others. High-pitched voices drowned out the opposition.

"You're crazy, you'll get us all shot!"

They called our latrine chief, a craven little man overwhelmed by the burden of his responsibility. Trembling with fear yet not daring to oppose our attempt, he started to argue but got nowhere as everyone began babbling at once and one woman began screaming hysterically.

"Call the guards, call the guards! Don't you see they want to have us all killed!"

The train had stopped. There was no need to call the guards;

the ruckus we were making had already drawn their attention. The outside panel blocking the barred windows slowly drew back and a scowling German face appeared.

"*Ruhe!*"

This bark was an order for silence. And we shut up. Again the train started up, and five or six of us tried to push in the floor until the chorus of protests resumed. We gave in then. Each of us went wearily back to his place.

We had given up because there was no way to silence these women and because we were so tired. Nervous exhaustion, the burning need for sleep, the compulsion just to creep back to our corners and rest, had sapped our determination. Toward evening I summoned up enough energy to go and test the floor, but it was no longer possible to get at the spot. My fellow captives had cautiously piled suitcases on top of it. It was too late.

As the second day passed, tempers frayed and morale continued to deteriorate. We were consumed by thirst. Yet despite our parched throats, a thick and gluey saliva filled our mouths. We who had food shared with the empty-handed our hard bread, unappetizing occupation bread which had become even less appetizing under the circumstances. There were also some cookies that prisoners had received from their families before leaving, and they were understandably willing to share them as they had become inedible. Still we ate them, devoured every crumb of everything. There was no more food, but lack of food was the least of our sufferings.

There was the ever more intolerable stench of sweat, filth, and excrement. And we would have given anything for a glass of water, but there wasn't even anyone to ask for it. On and on the train rolled, hour by hour making its rhythmical clickety-clack, on and on inexorably. At its infrequent stops we would hear the usual station noises, plus phrases in German, and sometimes whole conversations. Now we were getting deeper into enemy territory.

On the afternoon of the third day, while we were stopped at a small station, the freight car door suddenly opened. Probably they had just opened two or three cars at random as a sort of spot check. Anyway, armed soldiers stared up at us from the platform. Despite them three or four of us climbed out, irresistibly attracted to some water faucets we saw there. The soldiers didn't stop us getting out and allowed us to drink. Then we few men formed a human chain, passing bottles back to supply the people in our car. We worked fast as cries had gone up from prisoners seeing us from other cars, and now the soldiers rushed us back unceremoniously. In the process I got a terrible swipe across the ribs with a gun butt.

"*Los, los!*"

The door clanged shut on our car. Most of us, but not all, had been able to drink a little water. Those who had failed to get a sip whined and complained like children. And the children themselves cried because the little water they'd gotten hadn't even begun to quench their thirst. This mouthful of water, this unexpected bonanza in the midst of our distress, had solved nothing, had not refreshed us or improved the situation a whit. On the contrary, the pent-up bitterness that had been building up since the night before (and actually in fact since our departure) now came to a head. Now the merest trifle could cause a quarrel, one wrong word could bring on blows. A few of us not so hot-headed tried to separate quarrelers who started to fight, making them change their respective positions in the car. But even that was no easy matter—trying to arrange any kind of truce amidst that pile of stacked-up, ill bodies. About this time some of the prisoners began to hallucinate, seeing visions, mumbling, calling out and waving their arms.

That night I fell into deep sleep, but according to what my neighbor told me later, some women were assaulted. Not all of them had really tried to ward off their attackers. Some had put up a show of resistance which soon turned into sexual excitement. To me it seemed that only a sexually obsessed madman —or madwoman—could achieve any kind of gratification in this cesspool of horror.

The fourth day dawned on a herd of semicorpses, all prostrate on one another, utterly spent and half suffocated by the foul air. Our features were drawn, our eyes red. We were all leaden-faced, men with four-day stubble, women haggard and uncombed. So unendurable was our situation that we began to anticipate our forthcoming arrival as some sort of delivery.

That morning the door was thrown back and through the bars we saw a German soldier in a Wehrmacht steel helmet. He smiled, but the smile boded us no good. He had prudently decided to cash in on our arrival at this little station near Auschwitz; it was likely that such a steel-helmeted head had appeared in every freight-car window. He speedily made it known that he would not be averse to trading some black bread he had for whatever watches or jewels we had left.

Hardly anyone offered any protest at such an exchange, as most of us realized that in our circumstances a hunk of black bread was worth a good deal more than a gold watch. Also the soldier had brought along a jar of milk. He knew that there were always some children aboard these rolling cages. A terrible scene developed between two mothers about which of their crying babies should have the milk. Impassively, the clever merchant ignored the quarrel until it was resolved and he was paid for his milk and bread. Then he carefully examined his loot, holding the watches to his ear to see if they ticked. He seemed deaf to the pleas coming from every car.

"*Wasser, Wasser!*"

What would he get out of bringing us water? He walked off as our cries pursued him.

"Son of a bitch! Dirty Kraut! Robber!" etc.

And again the train started up. We had no way of knowing that these were to be our last few hours on the train. We no longer hoped for an end to this anguish, nor did we even stir at the sounds of confused hubbub at the end of the car. Apparently a woman had tried to commit suicide. At least that was the word that filtered back to us, and they asked us to call the guards. What had she done? We couldn't see anything, we could hear very little, we only knew that it was impossible to get to where she was. Confused bits of information were relayed back to us. We could only hear faint shrieks from the poor creature who had broken down. Finally her cries ceased.

The train slowed to a halt. Then followed much maneuvering as our long string of wooden cars drew up to a platform with one last shuddering jolt. Doors rolled open, this time wide. And we didn't stop to ask ourselves if this was the end of our journey. Groaning, pushing, and shoving, we made for the exit and the open air.

"*'Raus!* Outside! Get down, leave your baggage!"

The first frightened descenders disobeyed and tried to bring suitcases, which were instantly seized from their hands by guards. And now men in striped prison uniforms climbed onto the freight cars to oust the occupants with whips. Screaming like madmen, striking with all their strength, they showed no leniency to the crying babies and children. These men were themselves Auschwitz prisoners.

"*Schneller, schneller!* Faster!"

But how could we possibly move faster? We were stampeding each other, crazed by this unexpected ferocity. Women gasped and choked under the rain of blows, trying in vain to shelter their children. After being hit several times my shoulder hurt too much for me to ward off the blows effectively. Off we clambered, joined by the other cars' terrified occupants. Now the entire convoy from Drancy was assembled on the platform at Auschwitz.

In what a deplorable state! Later I learned that many had died en route.

I looked around for familiar faces and finally spotted a family I'd known in Paris who were desperately trying to keep together. What good would it do! Orders would soon separate them again.

A French-speaking S.S. officer directed operations. His shouting assistants quickly separated the mob according to a system known to all deportees. They put all ambulatory adults in one group. The other group consisted of all the rest—the children, the old people, those who for one reason or another could no longer walk. From the first group one column was formed of the men; another was made up of the women, who were sent walking in a different direction. The weak were simply loaded into trucks, in some cases thrown in.

The grouping operation was done with commendable dispatch and coordination. As our men's column started to march off, the prisoners in the striped uniforms finished piling the suitcases onto wheelbarrows.

5 NACHT UND NEBEL

As yet we had no conception of what Auschwitz was all about. We thought it might be something like old-time forced labor, but perhaps a little harsher since we were enemies of the state who had to be punished, and the majority of us were Jewish. But our imaginations went no further.

For many years, Hitler's propaganda machine had referred to "reeducation centers." Internees there were not supposed to be maltreated, much less killed, but simply brought to see the light by natural methods. Work, sports, and a healthy outdoor life in the country were supposed to work wonders toward bringing them to their senses. We clung to this happy belief despite ever increasing evidence to the contrary. The fact was that the mere idea of genocide could not be grasped readily by a so-called civilized European. Mass murder as official government policy was simply unthinkable. As indeed it still is; even today there are those who remain unconvinced that there ever was a Nazi extermination policy. Or perhaps it's simply that they don't want to hear about anything so appalling.

Anyway, we civilized Europeans realized that we had been condemned to forced labor. We also expected that some of us might be shot. But never did we contemplate systematic extermination—an idea that had occurred to Hitler back in 1939;

its execution he entrusted to the powerful S.S. organization.

But we prisoners still labored under the delusion that a human being must be respected as such—even conquered prisoners deprived of all rights and condemned to death were admittedly human. People like me who had been tortured by the Gestapo could rationalize that such exceptional treatment had been reserved for those who had actively worked against the Nazis in wartime. We none of us had a suspicion that we would be beaten every day like dogs and that we would reach such a point that a mere blow could be mortal.

Nor could our treatment be considered exactly slavery. For throughout history it was in the slaveowners' interest to keep their slaves alive. The Nazis had no such motivation, since in reviving the custom of slavery they did it with the difference that they *wanted* their slaves to die. After all, they were never threatened with a shortage of forced manpower.

Despite a constant expansion of the camps, which became numerous and vast enough to accommodate millions of internees, there was never enough room. Barracks always needed to be emptied to make room for new captives. So in order to empty the barracks they resorted to slaughter and cremation.

To say that we were deprived of our most elementary rights would be a rank understatement. Not only were we deprived of our rights, we were deprived of our conscience and constrained to infamy. Few of us succeeded in maintaining our humanity, few remained loyal to friends. Most learned to grovel, betray, lie, and steal. Practically all the survivors of prison camps refuse to talk about their past as internees, and this is less due to memories of suffering than to the recollection of their lost honor—an unbearable thought best to avoid altogether.

But at this point, as they drew us up into columns of five to lead us to the Auschwitz-Birkenau camp, we were still men. Ill and weak to be sure, but still men. For the blows raining down on us still had the power to rouse our indignation, and we angrily protested when the soldiers marching beside us tried to take our watches or rings. In pidgin French they tried to tell us that once in the camp, everything would be taken away. A few of the prisoners surrendered their watches in the mistaken belief that these soldiers would be their keepers and that it would be a good idea to keep in their good graces.

In the end it didn't matter. Upon reaching our destination, after three or four kilometers on the road, we were turned over to the kapos. After that it only took a few days for us to realize once and for all that we were no longer men.

Immediately on arrival we were stripped naked as jaybirds. Idiotically we tried to keep our scraps of clothing together, thinking maybe they would be labeled and given back later— a ridiculous hope, it turned out. Everything was taken away, including married men's wedding rings and the little chains that some wore around their necks. Shivering in the biting wind, we instinctively tried to cover our nakedness—one of the last instinctive reflexes as normal men we were to know. Even then, the feeling of shame over our nudity was soon supplanted by a piercing awareness of the freezing wind, the rain trickling over our skins, and the mud we were standing in.

Now it was time for another winnowing process. We queued up to pass before a doctor in a white tunic. He saw that some of us were not fit specimens at all. What had not been visible under cover of clothing now became undeniable in the full light of day. Hollow chests, bowed legs, muscular deficiencies, and hernias. Trembling, these physical rejects were led away, never to be seen again. They were killed, I later learned, along with those perfectly healthy men who had asked at the train station to travel in the trucks with the invalids. As punishment for their disinclination to walk, they were put to death the first day.

Once this medical inspection was over, they shaved every hair off our bodies. A team of barbers sheared us from head to foot: chest, pubic hair, testicles, and behind. We had to get on our haunches, spread our thighs, and go through a variety of humiliating postures. The men who shaved us were themselves shaved prisoners wearing the so-called pajamas; they worked silently with careful intentness. As my barber was French, I asked him confidentially what the camp was like.

"Bah, you'll see," he grunted.

I insisted, whereupon he remarked dispassionately that everyone here died like fleas. With a lot of luck I might be able to nab a soft job but I shouldn't count on it; a soft job was almost impossible to find and easy to lose. Generally an inmate at Auschwitz lasted about three months. But then he felt my boxer's muscles.

"You," he said, "might last a little longer—but not much."

He added that he expected to be going back to the work party soon and he wouldn't put up any fight, he was half dead already.

I couldn't take this in. The man was not joking, nor did he seem worried. He just seemed to have lost interest in everything. I begged him to tell me more, but he only shrugged, turning to the next customer. My time was up.

We all lined up for a shower, first with scalding water then suddenly freezing. We had to move quickly. A kapo (a German convict in charge of other prisoners) armed with a bludgeon screamed at us in German, sometimes kicking a bare backside. Teeth chattering, we tried to dry ourselves, all with the same wet meager towel.

I suddenly saw my friend Abastados, whom I'd worked out with many a time in the Paris gyms and seen again at Drancy. A physical-culture buff, he had the magnificent body of a Greek statue. Within two weeks he was dead.

Next our serial numbers were tattooed on our forearms and we were told that we must learn them in German.

We were then dressed, that is to say we were thrown scraps of clothing: a shirt, a cap, wooden clogs, and the famous blue and gray striped pajamas of a concentration camp inmate. The shirt was in tatters, the cap came in various different shapes, the wooden shoes cut our feet cruelly. Naturally the pajamas seldom fit and we tried to swap among ourselves as best we could. As most buttons were missing we did what we could to hold the garments together with bits of string or anything we could find. This simple project turned out to require a good deal of trouble and time. What you needed was never around, nothing could ever be found right away.

Once more we were assembled in a completely barren barracks, where we slept on the ground floor. It appeared that we were still in quarantine. Newcomers were not put to work immediately; a few days were needed to indoctrinate them and prepare them for existence in the camp.

During this waiting period I encountered my friend Henri Bulawko, who had arrived in the same convoy. At the sight of each other we burst out laughing, for we seemed grotesquely decked out for some weird carnival. We were grotesque not so much because of our strange garb in itself but because of the contrast with our healthy faces. Despite what we'd been through and even with our shaved heads, we still looked fairly normal—too normal to match our scarecrow attire. The faces of the few long-term prisoners we had seen were appropriately sunken, gray, and drawn. They looked tragic, pathetic, poignant, but they were not grotesque.

I repeated to Henri what the barber had said. He replied that he too had heard the same story but that it must be exaggerated.

An average survival span of three months in the camps? Incredible! Conditions might be tough, but after all, prison was prison. The idea that the Germans could wantonly destroy us seemed absurd. Why would they deliberately deprive themselves of free manpower? So reasoned Henri, echoing at least a hundred voices I'd heard previously.

Now a first column of prisoners, drawn up like soldiers, marched toward the camp and crossed the barbed-wire barrier. Other columns joined them to assume positions in the open spaces between the barracks. When they passed a guard post where the S.S. were stationed, they automatically doffed their caps. On they marched through the central area, halting before the barracks.

For over an hour we newcomers sat there and watched the roll-call check of men returning from their labors. Exact numbers were carefully kept in the camp register. Once all the prisoners were drawn up in perfect formation and standing at attention, they were counted and recounted by kapos armed with clubs.

By this time night had long fallen, yet these human wrecks on the verge of collapse had to stand at attention until the last man had been counted. Some distance away near the barbed wire a spit-and-polish S.S. officer in shining boots held the leash of two fierce police dogs.

When the prisoners were finally dismissed and allowed to return to their barracks, Henri and I overcame our fatigue enough to reconnoiter, hoping to run into a familiar face or two. But we had no luck at all. Not a soul did we see of our former Drancy campmates who had endured the train ride with us.

It was true, of course, that Birkenau was merely one segment of the monstrous complex known as Auschwitz. The enslaved men around us who nightly stumbled into the barracks for their meager fare of margarine-dotted bread did not even speak our language. A mixed lot of Russians, Poles, Czechs, and Hungarians, they were all stonily indifferent to us who'd come to join their hard lot. Long ago they had run out of sympathy. What was one more wave of prisoners! Now the main concern of these seasoned prisoners seemed to be to chew their hunks of black bread as long as possible. After their thorough chewing they would form little groups to chat desultorily for a while before falling on their bunks to sleep.

When eventually we did find some Frenchmen in one of the barracks, they were total strangers to us.

None of them was from Drancy; some had been caught in the provinces and some hailed from Algeria and Morocco. They shrugged when we asked for news of our acquaintances. They knew nothing about our friends, but they did enlighten us as to the scope of this vast Nazi operation—the wholesale slaughter as well as the inexorable mechanics of destruction. Auschwitz with its dependent camps was like a teeming city with a floating, constantly changing population. One of the men painfully arose and led us into the courtyard to point out a far-off sight we hadn't noticed—the smokestacks of the crematoriums with their plume of flame and smoke. And the pungent odor that we smelled occasionally when the wind shifted, which we hadn't identified but were henceforth to smell daily—that was the smell of burning human flesh.

This man proved well informed. He explained to us that seventy-five to eighty percent of all the new arrivals to Auschwitz—those unfit for manual labor—were immediately exterminated. After all, most were unfit because by the time they reached this place they had already been through a great deal. And so right away the old, the infirm, cripples, women with babes in arms, small children, and undersized youths were bundled onto trucks and speedily driven to a certain barracks which resembled one of the shower houses but was in fact a gas chamber. A picked group directed the slayings. Called the Sonderkommando, these executioners theoretically lived apart and had no contact with the other staff. Nevertheless word got about. The condemned—men, women, and children together—were stripped completely, then locked in an airtight room into which poisonous gas was piped. After which the Sonderkommando had the task of extracting the corpses' gold teeth, cutting off the women's hair, and carting the bodies to the crematorium.

Birkenau ovens were inadequate though their chimneys spat flames night and day, said our informant, adding that he himself had seen funeral pyres—enormous ditches belching fire. There were always more corpses than the crematoriums could handle.

Thus it was that we got to know the awful truth about our situation. This was what they had told us in France and what we'd refused to believe, and now we would soon be a part of the massacre. Henri and I looked at each other, our eyes wide with anxiety.

Our fellow prisoner spared us no illusions. Yes, he went on, we too would die here, for the day was bound to come when we couldn't work any longer. Overworked, half starved, and ill treated, the so-called Moslems, having no further function at camp, were put an end to by the time they'd been reduced to skeletal condition. It was inevitable. Of course if you were a very, very smart operator, and hustled a soft job, and if the war finished soon . . .

That was it! Eagerly we snatched at that straw, the war ending in time to save us. The Russians might come! Auschwitz was in Poland, after all! Maybe Germany surrounded would soon collapse! In other words, our will to live still blazed brightly.

Later, though, back in our barracks and lying on the wet ground where we tried vainly to sleep, we had to admit that our chances were slim: already our trainload had been cut to one fifth its original size. According to one of our people, who had counted the freight cars when we left, there were originally fifteen hundred of us. Now only two hundred men remained in our column. The women and children they'd sent off in another direction might account for another hundred. There was that second screening to take into consideration.

Husbands and fathers in the quarantine barracks had no inkling that at that very moment their wives and children were being consumed by the flames.

The longer Henri and I stayed awake, the more outlandish our optimism of a few hours ago appeared. It now seemed that in the long run, those who had voluntarily climbed into the trucks at the Auschwitz station to spare themselves the walk had chosen the best way out! Why try to avoid the gas chamber today only to arrive there one, two, or three months later after a lot of pain and suffering? Was this extra little bit of life worth the trouble? Wouldn't it be wiser now to throw ourselves against the barbed wire we'd heard was electrified? The question implied more than the personal one of whether or not to put an end to our misery. There was also our common interest, the cause we'd fought for. At this point, accepting life might

be a betrayal of that cause. For there could be no doubt that
the Germans intended to make us work for them. Whether in
the mines or in the factories we would be directly supporting
the German war effort, and the arms we would help make
would be used to destroy what we had fought to defend.

Lying side by side, chilled to the bone, we could hear our
companions thrashing about in their sleep. All of us, day or
night, wore the evil-smelling convict pajamas worn by many
others before us. Their seams cut into our flesh. But we had to
get used to them just as we must get used to our shaven bodies,
our tattooed arms, our hunger, and our exhaustion.

6 ARBEIT MACHT FREI

FOR twenty-three months I wore the striped uniform of the convict. I served two months at Birkenau, three months at Jaworzno (another Auschwitz annex), fourteen months at the main camp of Auschwitz itself, and the rest in Mauthausen and Gusen II.

Except for brief periods of quarantine and rare visits to the "dream house," or infirmary, I worked continuously—like a beast of burden, I started to say, except that a beast of burden is not necessarily always being harassed as we were.

Over the gate at Auschwitz there was a surrealistic sort of metallic sign outlined against the gray sky: *Arbeit Macht Frei* —Work Makes One Free! I never knew if it was a sick joke or serious Nazi propaganda for passersby.

In the course of these twenty-three months I did every kind of dirty job. I hauled tree trunks on my shoulders. I mined coal in the bowels of the earth and I pushed heavy loaded carts up steep slopes. I shaped pieces of sheet metal on wooden forms. I made seats for machine gunners' assistants. I helped assemble an electric power plant, staggering through the swamp mud. I dug ditches in mine galleries. I cleaned latrines. I loaded the corpses of my comrades onto barrows.

And all this on a practically empty stomach! I always felt

faint from lack of food. For months on end I suffered from dysentery; also, my feet and hands were usually bloody. I had a chronic cough, perpetually running sores, and frostbite.

Fortunately for me I had started out strong as an ox, and so was able to fight discouragement. Also, as I've said, I knew how to adapt, how to use the defense reflexes which permitted me to duck or endure blows, just as professional boxers dodge and receive them. Above all, though, Lady Luck was on my side.

By great good fortune I was spared long stints at the worst camps (only two months at Birkenau, most notorious of the whole Auschwitz complex) and the deadliest work camps (I left Jaworzno's coal mine after three months; I doubt if anyone ever held out there longer).

Again, sheer luck kept me out of the path of the more murderous S.S. and kapos. Twenty blows duly meted out by someone a little heavy-handed could easily kill anyone in our weakened condition. Angry S.S. officers often killed in a fit of temper. Had I encountered one of these types it would have been all over for me, as I was punished quite a lot, more than most prisoners, receiving my full due of twenty-five lashes with a bullwhip during a so-called athletic session. Often on such occasions a spark of hate sufficed to turn twenty-five lashes into an assassination.

My luck held too with the doctors. Sometimes these physicians prescribed death for weak patients, and sometimes they selected twelve healthy men to be experimented on. The human guinea pigs were castrated, given shots to acquire various diseases, frozen, operated on without anesthetics, etc. None of these men was ever seen again.

Twice as I faced death, destiny provided Nazi saviors for me—men who happened to be interested in boxing.

A long chain of happenstance, one coincidence after another, carried me through to the end—not unscathed by a long shot, but still alive. Out of all the other prisoners, only a handful could say the same.

The day after my group arrived at Birkenau we were given

our first indoctrination to prepare us for life in the concentration camp. Our mentors were a kapo, assisted by his male secretary. First off, we learned that we were to address them by their exact titles of Blockältester and Blockschreiber. The kapo was a German ex-convict who had been condemned well before the war, not for opposing the Nazi regime, but for murder. He spoke only German. His assistant the Schreiber smoothly translated the odious instructions. And this assistant, I regret to say, was French.

The first day, standing at attention and listening to the monotonous voice of the Schreiber, I made the mistake of shifting my weight a bit to ease the strain on my legs. Instantly the kapo rushed over to hit me in the face, so hard that I reeled and almost lost consciousness. Henceforth I understood what he meant about standing at attention.

Here is more or less what I learned at Birkenau in the first few days of quarantine. I have written the instructions down as well as I can remember them, but I cannot reproduce the hate that accompanied them, the scornful expression and contemptuous tone.

"You are now in the camp of Auschwitz-Birkenau. Get this well into your thick head. You are in a concentration camp. Don't think for a moment that you have been brought here simply to relax. A concentration camp is not a sanatorium. You will not be served breakfast in bed and you will not have a maid to clean up after you.

"You will have to work! You will have to handle pick and shovel, you will have to carry heavy burdens. You will have to obey promptly the kapos in charge of work parties. Prisoners who do their work properly should have no cause for worry. They will be left alone. But those who show the slightest indolence or resistance to orders should beware! We allow for no infractions of the rules. Those who fail to work properly will be made to lower their trousers and to receive twenty-five lashes, those who engage in sabotage will be hanged.

"Here you must respect the chiefs. The chiefs are your

superiors. Beside them you are less than a lump of shit. You will execute your chief's orders immediately. When you hear the word *Aufstehen,* you will jump up immediately without a second's delay. If you arrive late at roll call you will be punished. When you are told *Antreten,* you will line up without wasting a second. In formation, stand up straight and in neat rows, your hands down at your sides, your heads up, looking neither right nor left. When you hear *Mützen ab,* you will smartly take off your cap, slapping your hand against your thigh. And when you hear *Mützen auf,* you will put it back on your head. Those failing to execute these commands properly should beware: they will be punished. When you leave the camp to go to work, you will salute as ordered, and you will salute in the same way when you come back.

"You must also learn to dress properly. A convict cannot be allowed to look like a pig. He must wash and take care of his uniform and shoes. Uniform and shoes are very important. Look to it that they are not stolen. If you lose your shoes, you will march barefoot, and if you lose your cap or your pants you will receive twenty-five lashes.

"Keep yourselves clean. Those filthy swine who fail to do so will be chastised with a club until they learn better. And beware of fleas. It is a graver offense to have fleas than it is to do sabotage work. Those who have fleas will be sent to the gas chambers and they will die along with their fleas.

"You will have to learn German to understand orders. If you do not understand you cannot execute them. You will have to learn your serial number by heart and be able to say it in German whenever you are asked. If you don't you will be punished. Here you have no name; instead you have a number. You must learn it by heart and say it without hesitation and without any mistake, and when your number is called do not pretend to misunderstand or to have forgotten it.

"Do not try to escape for it is impossible. No one has ever escaped from a concentration camp. If you try you will be caught and you will be hanged immediately. And you will not get more than a kilometer away before you are caught. Also, those of you who have played any part whatsoever in the plot or know of it and have not warned the chiefs will be hanged. It is absolutely impossible to escape from a concentration camp.

"Don't try to approach the barbed wire. There is a boundary line which you should not try to pass. If you venture beyond it by so much as half an inch, the sentinel will shoot without warning and you will be executed.

"Remember that you are in a concentration camp here. A concentration camp is not a sanatorium."

It didn't take us long to realize that the kapo's speech was no idle threat, but if anything an understatement. Indeed the horror of the camp far exceeded our worst nightmares; we had to follow the kapo's advice to the letter if we wanted to preserve any'cnance at all of surviving.

Assiduously we practiced the *Mützen ab* and the *Mützen auf*, the first important item in the regulations. It was not so easy as it looked. Mützen came in all shapes and sizes, which made getting them on and off in a hurry a bit tricky. The hat had to fit tightly but not too tightly if the maneuver was to be done precisely. Anyone clumsy enough to drop his cap while saluting was sure to be severely punished. So was anyone who lost his clogs while in ranks. They pinched, and could only be kept on by clenching your big toes.

The trouble was that try as you might to obey the rules, you could still be punished. A little awkwardness or distraction and you'd broken the cadence of motion. That meant you'd had it! Being German, the kapos naturally had a reverential respect for military rhythm, and any sloppiness on our part made them see red. Besides, they knew how to command and knew they'd be demoted for any hint of weakness. A kapo who fell from grace and got demoted to being an ordinary prisoner again was a dead duck; his former subordinates would see to that. Revenge was sweet and they were inexorable. They clobbered the stumblers, raining blows on heads and shoulders. Some kapos used a club, but most preferred a sand-filled rubber hose called a *Gummi*.

Being tardy to roll call was an unpardonable crime. One day a prisoner reached his group a moment after the others and tried to slip into the ranks unobserved. He was only a few seconds late. But the eagle-eyed kapo saw. He crooked a finger indicating that the fellow should come to him.

"Komm her, komm her."

The unfortunate man blanched, hesitated, and began to stammer. *"Komm!"*

He left the ranks and approached the smiling kapo. Just as he was taking off his cap, the Gummi came crashing down on his shaven head. He staggered, and a second blow sent him to the ground. The kapo leaned down, hoisted him up, waited until he opened his eyes, and then struck even more viciously than before.

At last when the man lay quite motionless, the kapo called to another kapo in a nearby group. Placing the Gummi across the victim's throat, the two kapos stood together on it, their full weight on each end of the weapon. We could hear a snapping noise.

From the front rank I watched with horror. My neighbor and I were given the order to remove the body. We had to put it in the barracks so that it could be present at roll call that evening. Even the dead had to be there at roll call.

Subsequently, I was to witness this form of murder scores of times.

I saw some who died at the first stroke of the club, their skulls cracked or their vertebrae crushed. And I saw other victims of a beating who raved delirious on their beds until morning before dying. Hearts in feeble bodies could not withstand prolonged brutality.

I began to see that the kapos did not necessarily choose their victims. To be sure, they did punish faults and they did often strike when they didn't like the looks of a prisoner. But mostly, they struck at random—first because it was their duty to keep the prisoners permanently terrified and second because they enjoyed doing it.

Kapos had power of life and death over us. Nearly all were German, common criminals let loose from the Reich's penitentiaries where they had served for years before being transferred to the concentration camps. Many had been at Auschwitz since its very beginning. They helped build the camp and they wore the oldest serial numbers. Some were Jewish, and they were no less ferocious than the rest. Their ferocity, like that of the others, stemmed partly from necessity, as any relenting would have meant the loss of their privileged position.

In theory kapos were given twice as much to eat as the others; in actuality they had *all* they wanted to eat, nor was their food the same foul mess doled out to their charges. The kapos formed a gang in the vast Auschwitz area and operated every imaginable racket. They had their own little Mafia, selling, buying, trading, hoarding, and robbing through intimidation. They established trade channels within and without the camp; made deals with civil servants inside the warehouse; catalogued the items taken from the gassed prisoners: their clothes, fur coats, jewelry, and gold fillings and crowns. "Organization" meant negotiating on the kitchen supplies, to the further reduction of prisoners' rations. Kapos also made deals with those who made use of the camp's labor force—German companies and a neighboring Polish peasant.

The S.S. couldn't have cared less how the rackets worked, for however money was made they got the lion's share. They delegated the camp's administration to the kapos, and only rarely were to be seen at all. Busy with their financial affairs, their games, and their brothels, these lords appeared infrequently among us, generally to make an example of some particular offender or to supervise the weeding-out process.

A brothel was set up at Auschwitz, patronized mostly by the S.S., plus a few privileged kapos. A fresh supply of girls came from every trainload of new arrivals. They never lasted long, due to the atrocious and perverted demands to which they were subjected. Naturally there was no question of prisoners going there. Not that they were any longer capable of sexual desire, ravaged as they were by ill treatment, malnutrition, and dysentery. Many who survived the camps never regained their virility.

Prisoners mostly had one desire and one only—food. Their dreams centered on what gorgeous feasts they would order if they could. Many an hour was spent of an evening planning banquet menus and occasionally swapping recipes. Food! We never tired of discussing it.

The well-fed kapos, on the other hand, fit and athletic from the daily workout they inflicted on their charges, concentrated all their pleasures on sex. These sadists satisfied themselves in dreadful ways. Usually they found it convenient to adopt a catamite among the young prisoners. All the time he was being buggered he was given extra food and a soft job. But he couldn't count on survival for long. Once the "peoples," as they were called, ceased to whet their masters' jaded appetites, they were tossed onto the scrap heap, soon to perish.

From time to time, on various jobs, I would glimpse women's work teams in the distance. At Auschwitz, women really were the frailer sex, even more dehumanized by their experience than men. Dressed like us in striped uniforms, they tied rags over their shaven heads. And like us, they marched to work in columns of five, in step and singing. It was incongruous to hear these dying, emaciated females sing German marching songs that were so gay and lively. They marched along, driven on by whip-waving female kapos shouting orders.

I only saw these women a few times, and never got to have a conversation with them. Yet some men did. Some clandestine meetings between the sexes did occur, despite all precautions.

Our diet, which never varied an iota in the world of concentration camps, consisted of the following: morning, a mug of hot colored water dignified by the name of coffee; at noon a quart of soup; and at night a chunk of black bread, sometimes but not always with a bit of sausage or margarine. This little piece of black bread was our staple. Rations ran from two to three hundred grams. Black crude bread, often moldy, but it was our only regular food. Some of the prisoners had crude knives they had patiently fashioned from bits of sharpened steel, and they sliced the bread thinly to make it seem like more.

You had to keep a sharp eye out. Some men suffered the pangs of hunger more than others, and they hung around stealthily awaiting the chance to steal. You couldn't drop your guard for a moment: like ferrets they would seize any unwatched morsel and scurry to a corner with it. Such pilfering often resulted in fights, which the kapos stopped by striking about indiscriminately, as if they were subduing a pack of wild dogs. When these starved wretches found nothing to steal, they would wander toward the kitchens in the hope of scavenging peels among the garbage. They would eat anything. I frequently joined these evening excursions. Very frequently.

The noonday soup was made of boiled rutabagas and carrots. Occasionally one might find a visible piece of potato in it. But only a tiny percentage consisted of solid vegetables; a quart of soup was mainly a quart of water. Even so, we were eager for it. In the middle of a hard day's work, this soup provided relaxation and a little comfort. It was generally insipid and sometimes foully bitter, but we still wanted it. We had to form a proper line and remain alert to get it, for the ladle could just as easily land on the victim's head, or the soup simply be poured onto the ground, and he would lose his ration.

I even saw one furious S.S. officer grab a poor wretch by the shoulders and drown him by soaking his head in a tubful of soup. It happened that I was on KP with this unfortunate man; our job was to run between the kitchens, picking up the two-handled basins filled with boiling liquid. It was a good job, as it enabled us to sneak a little extra food. But on this occasion, tragically, my companion tripped over some obstacle and let go of the handle, so that a little soup spilled out. It was only a ladle or two of soup wasted, yet fate had it that just then one of the dread S.S. was crossing the courtyard, and saw the loss. At once in a towering rage, he rushed across shouting imprecations, grabbed my poor companion, and bent the man's head into the basin.

There was a squeal of fear, a brief struggle, gurgles and weak kicks, then the prisoner no longer moved. Dropping the limp body to the earth, the S.S. strode off, dabbing with his handkerchief at a few drops of soup on his sleeve.

I witnessed this murder in the same manner that I witnessed many others—with an expressionless face and standing rigidly at attention. Had I spoken one word of protest, much less tried to help the victim, I too would have been murdered.

I used our so-called morning coffee—about half a pint of beige-colored hot water—to wash. I applied it to my face, and very soothing it was, especially in winter. Some poor devils used to put their penises in their coffee to soak them for solace, the lack of hygiene and psychological misery having swollen them to a painful degree.

Occasionally I was able to hustle a little extra food—meager and rare, but it helped keep me going. Once or twice I had a neat stroke of luck. For instance, there was a generous British prisoner, employed as worker in one of the armament factories, who kindly gave me some of the goodies that he as a Britisher was entitled to receive from home. For a few days, with that little extra, I felt almost well fed. Another time, not so lucky, a Polish civilian gave me a little tobacco as thanks for some help I'd given him. This tobacco, equal almost to two packs of cigarettes, would have allowed me to eat for days by bartering, but sadly, I never got to use it.

We were searched that day—we often were in the ranks—and the S.S. who found it slapped me twice, violently, and crammed the tobacco into his pocket. Had he been in the mood, he could have killed me with his bare hands right then.

It was a mild punishment, but, I felt, an irreparable loss.

Compared to Birkenau, the main camp at Auschwitz could have been considered bearable. For Birkenau was the absolute pit of horror and depravity. Thousands of half-dead men were piled into a permanently vile-smelling barracks. Latrines consisted simply of deep trenches where the excrement was allowed to stack up. Inside the barracks tubs were used for the same purpose. Occasionally, men would collapse into these from faintness. More often, squatting prisoners were shoved deep into the tubs by some passing S.S. with a macabre sense of humor. As a rule the butt of the joke could not climb out, no one dared help him, and so he died there, crying.

Unquestionably Birkenau had the very highest extermination rate. Its four ovens, built in 1942, were inadequate despite the addition of funeral pyres. Every new trainload called for additional slaughter, since room always had to be made for the newest trainloads of victims. Crowding reached such a point in the three-decker bunks that prisoners literally slept one atop the other. Often they smothered. Every day, corpses were taken from the dormitories and work sites.

Though the food and work were no better at Auschwitz, at least housing was much improved. We slept in one-story brick barracks whose walls had been painted in bright colors, and these at least boasted washbasins and WCs.

There were about eighty-five barracks, each holding a thousand men under average circumstances, and at times nearly twice that many. The minimal cleanliness we achieved in these buildings doubtless had much to do with reducing mortality. Furthermore, there were even periods when the system notably relaxed. A new superior S.S. officer taking command of the camp might decree an end to brutality, and except for disciplinary action, violence would stop for a few weeks.

But the respite never lasted, and in any case it did not prevent famine and exhaustion from doing their work. The gas chambers and ovens had to have their share of victims, the weeding-out process went on as always.

Work parties marched to and from the job accompanied

by sprightly music. At first the phenomenon amazed me, the sight of these pathetic slaves marching off to jolly martial airs. But even more grotesquely, hangings were carried out to the strains of music.

Thus at least twice a day, and oftener on special occasions, we were treated to band concerts. The orchestra played on a makeshift dais not far from the main gate. Like ourselves the musicians were pajama-clad prisoners, though not quite so cadaverous. They played classical waltzes, military marches, and the latest popular songs. Thanks to their performance, the work parties could step smartly en route to their labors, and at execution time music created the proper ceremonial atmosphere.

I never got acquainted with these musicians, most of whom were Hungarian, and some, it seemed, well-known artists in their own countries. In addition to their orchestral chores, they were probably employed as Stubendienst—janitors or something of the kind. In general their lot was not as bad as ours, though of course they breathed the same foul air, had the same melancholy look, the same gray skin and empty eyes. The conductor mechanically waved his arms like a wooden doll. At the finale they would gloomily pack up their instruments and march off in unison.

Why this music? we often asked ourselves. We wondered too about the beautifully tended flowerbeds around so many of the barracks. Perhaps the music and the flowers attested to that romantic aspect of the German soul that no horror could diminish.

The drastic contrast of Birkenau's filth and stench with the cleanliness and even beauty of Auschwitz was a paradox that we prisoners never even tried to fathom. To be sure, precious few of the inmates stayed alive long enough to make any comparisons, the great majority dying of starvation and deprivation very soon.

Anyway, no amount of music and landscaping prevented our having lice. Regularly, from time to time, we were assembled for Laus Kontrol—lice inspection—a serious matter, as those guilty of harboring vermin were severely punished.

Every inch of our bare bodies was scrutinized, especially our armpits and between our legs. We dreaded this inspection, but worse was to come when typhoid struck. Those afflicted with the disease were ruthlessly quarantined, if that is the word: they were dumped naked, without food or treatment, into a ward and left quite alone. They died by the hundreds. Every morning a work party would come load the corpses onto wheelbarrows; a few survived, thanks to devoted friends who dared to slip into the sickroom and bring them food and water.

In camp slang, men who had reached the nadir of weakness and emaciation were called Moslems. I became a Moslem when I dropped to seventy-seven pounds (from a normal weight of 155). And it was entirely possible to dwindle even below this point to become literally skin and bones. Our ribs could be easily counted, our jawbones jutted through our cheeks, wrinkled skin hung in folds from our thighs.

All entangled together in the ditches, the naked dead looked strangely like snakes. The sight did not faze us, accustomed as we were to horror, but it repelled the first American soldiers who liberated us later at Gusen II.

Periodically a German military doctor would wander among the prisoners and select some for execution. He made a quick appraisal, then noted down the serial numbers of the chosen ones. Those whose numbers appeared on this list knew well what was in store. They never tried to argue or protest, nor did they seem afraid. So utterly exhausted were they, so drained by this time, that any emotion was beyond them. Yet they mustered the strength to stagger to their feet and form ranks, for even here at the end order and discipline were required. Then they marched quietly off to their destiny.

I knew their numbed state of mind, for twice I was put on the blacklist. During the days or hours beforehand, I'd been tormented by fear, anxiety, self-pitying memories of my family. But when the moment actually arrived, when the orderly expressionlessly read out my number on the list, it came, oddly enough, as a relief. All over now! The end had come at last. No more uncertainty, no more stress, no more problems!

Once condemned, prisoners even felt an impatience to get it all over with; that was why, at the final moment, they could troop off without a tremble or a backward glance.

But how we struggled before reaching that point! We would try anything, any means, to avoid being put on the list. Health meant survival, and sometimes before the physical checkup, men would slap themselves violently in the hope of bringing a rosy flush to their sunken cheeks. The ruse never worked, for it was bodies, not faces, that the doctor looked at.

A few prisoners—though not as many as one might expect—wanted to hurry to death. They had little trouble finding it. Some at the end of their mental tether voluntarily joined the group of doomed men. Others would simply make a run for it, to be mowed down by machine guns in the watchtowers. And I heard of a coal miner who took an S.S. officer with him in his hundred-foot leap into the quarry where he worked.

For quite a while, I tried to assemble the nucleus of a Resistance group. Naturally I wasn't the only one to think of this—there were a few such willing partisans among every trainload from Poland, France, and Greece, and even among German political prisoners who shared our fate. Surely, I thought, we could establish a network to make contact with Polish Resistance fighters, or organize an escape. On a more modest scale, it seemed worthwhile to work out a system of mutual help within the camp itself—a cooperative scheme aimed at guaranteeing the survival of its associates. News of German setbacks had begun to filter down to us, mainly from the women's camp at Birkenau, which seemed to have the closest contact with the civilian population. More and more we heard of Axis defeats and the progress being made by Russian forces. Every day it seemed increasingly necessary for the prisoners to plan a last-minute revolt, an uprising to coincide with the breakthrough of Soviet forces. Otherwise the Nazis would finish us off to prevent our testifying against them.

But in vain we awaited an opportunity. In October of 1944, the Sonderkommando at the Birkenau crematoriums staged a gallant attack. All eight hundred executioners, mostly Jews from Poland and Hungary, formed a stable, united, and relatively privileged group. Always aware that inevitably they would have to be eliminated as the most deadly witnesses against the Nazis, these men dared to gamble. The Sonderkommando lost, but they did not die in vain. They were able to introduce a large quantity of explosive arms and munitions into the area around the crematoriums. On the night of the revolt we heard gunfire. Later we got the news that the eight hundred had managed to kill seventy S.S. men before they were wiped out.

Such a desperate venture remained quite impossible for most of us ordinary prisoners at Auschwitz—even during those relatively slack interims when the command changed. The shifting flux of prisoners, perpetually displaced and altered, lacked the minimum stability necessary.

Even from the beginning I had noticed the antagonism between nationalities, a mutual hostility which prevented any effective united effort. A successful revolt would depend on contacts and accomplices being maintained in every barracks —and we couldn't even form a group within the limited framework of a dormitory or work party! For one's daily companions were constantly disappearing. Hardly was a budding friendship begun when death or departure would end it. Intimacy takes a while to develop.

So we were denied the consolation of any true comradeship, any meeting of the minds with the new lot of strangers we were continually being confronted with.

We could not share our misery. Each of us felt as isolated and abandoned as if he were in solitary confinement. Each of us felt alien to all these strangers who were fellow prisoners.

We got on each other's nerves, snapped at one another, quarreled violently over trivialities, and fought teeth and nail over a crust of bread or a swallow of soup. Only a kapo's club could separate us.

Because we couldn't unite or even attain any kind of understanding, we lost souls could only obey our savage instinct to survive. Such was our withdrawn solitude, our intrinsic loathing for all humans including ourselves, that I frequently asked myself whether we could ever return to normal life in the event that we survived. At the time it seemed impossible. Our chronic unhappiness, mistrust, suspicion, and general neuroticism had long since divided us. Only the actual presence of our tormentors inclined us to cling together even momentarily.

And so we couldn't begin to consider any unified, organized resistance. At best, single acts of sabotage were possible on the rare occasions that our work situations permitted. More likely, we could simply shirk on the job; one might make the most of inadequate supervision or try to avoid it. Like others I did this whenever possible on whatever job they put me. Very often I managed to perform about a tenth of my allotted task, and sometimes was even able to undo it completely. However modest the result of my tactics may appear, and however much they were canceled by the inhuman pace at which we worked, I can still remain a little proud of this. I fought against the enemy as best I could.

7 A MINER AT JAWORZNO

THERE came a day at Jaworzno when I really hit bottom. This occurred three months after my arrival at the concentration camp. Lying inert on a bed at the infirmary, too weak to lift a finger voluntarily, I was awaiting my turn to be chosen for the gas chamber. Three months of misery had worn me out.

At Birkenau I'd begun my career as an unloader of logs. It was hard work, but in those days I still had all my strength. Two of us unloaded the heavy logs from a truck, carried them fifty yards, stacked them, and returned to the truck for more.

We kept this up for twelve consecutive hours daily always at top speed, except for the half hour we had off for soup and any moment we could snatch when the sharp-eyed Vorarbeiter wasn't looking.

Considering the diet we were on—about seven hundred calories a day—this grueling job was enough to kill a man very quickly. And all the time we labored the kapos kept striking us, each blow adding to our exhaustion.

I was on the point of collapse, my bruised shoulder raw from the logs and my feet deeply lacerated, when mercifully, I recognized one of the Stubendienst as an old acquaintance of mind.

The Stubendienst were in charge of cleaning rooms and

distributing food. Although they had to toil even harder than the rest of us—for their domestic duties didn't spare them outside jobs on a work site—they did get extra rations. And however poor the bread and thin the soup, getting enough of them increased the odds in your favor. Food dispensers with any talent for "organization" also had opportunities denied the others. As the trusted confidant of a Blockältester (the kapo in charge of a barracks) and as the link between him and the camp authorities, a clever Stubendienst could become the indispensable go-between for the thousand and one deals always brewing inside the camp. Of course, at the first sign of inefficiency he could lose his job and be sent back to rejoin the common herd of prisoners.

My Stubendienst acquaintance had known my family in Paris. He was easily recognizable, not having wasted away too badly by concentration camp standards. A two-hundred-pound man down to a hundred and thirty-five isn't nearly as thin as he can get, and this one seemed within the camp hierarchy to have the privileges of a first-class soldier. He had many useful contacts which he at once exploited on my behalf: he recommended me to a Vorarbeiter, or foreman in charge of a work gang. This particular group was building the foundations of a future power house, and they allowed me to join it.

I shall never forget the man who gave me my first real stroke of good luck at camp. (He is still alive.) He rescued me from the log-carrying and placed me on this work team, where I could only pretend to help, being woefully unskilled.

My foreman the Vorarbeiter had accepted me with some misgivings. After all, he was only a convict himself and under the orders of a kapo. And he was held responsible for the work turned out.

Yet a Vorarbeiter, like a Stubendienst, could be considered a favored convict likely to outlast the others, for his duty was to make the others work, rather than work himself. In order to secure such a job and hold it for any length of time he had to act as the kapo's second in command, which implied that he must acquire the kapo mentality as well as the kapo handiness with a club.

Somehow I was never awarded the honor and privilege of wearing a corporal's stripes, but those who did managed to survive as long as their stream of physical and mental abuse to the slave gang continued unabated. Any sign of their energies' flagging meant instant dismissal; they were broken back into the ranks after first being punished for their lapse with the standard twenty-five of the best on the behind, *fünfundzwanzig auf Arsch*.

The Vorarbeiter who reluctantly accepted me in his shop saw at once that I had only pretended to be a technician and that I had absolutely no acquaintance with even the commonest tools. But he let me stay, being falsely assured by my protector that I had the support of the Blockältester. He beat me as often as he did the others, but pulled his punches; one can always hold back the full strength of a blow just as the club reaches its target. Furthermore he gave me a job in a little dark corner, so that my incompetence could be less glaring.

Thus for ten or so tranquil days I escaped the hell of Birkenau and even enjoyed extra crusts of black bread by courtesy of my friend the Stubendienst. I am very much in his debt—perhaps for my life, as by the time of my inevitable expulsion from the oasis, I'd recovered some strength and the use of my legs. The grinding drudgery on the Holzplatz had just about ruined my feet. And to have bad feet was considered a heinous crime. The slightest limp made one appear unfit for arduous duty, which in turn led to the gas chamber. Limping in the ranks was inadmissible.

On my tenth day of loafing and recuperating I was spotted by the kapo responsible for that sector and unceremoniously kicked out. Fortunately no investigation was made of the fraud which had gotten me the job in the first place. I was called a pile of ordure and a whore's son, among other things, and I was beaten and kicked and then simply thrown out. But none of it was lethal and mere insults didn't faze me. Back I went to my log-carrying—as monotonous a job as it was painful.

It looked as though I might remain at this backbreaking project indefinitely—at least until I broke down—because I lacked any concrete skills. The little apprentice work I'd done in my turbulent youth hadn't provided a technical trade. I was a boxer first and last, in the stable of the famous trainer Jean Bretonnel, who predicted a brilliant future for me. Unfortunately there was no demand for boxers at Birkenau.

But as it turned out, I soon left the Holzplatz at Birkenau. It happened like this: an official body consisting of an S.S. officer, an army doctor, and two or three civilians from the outside world decided to look over us log-rollers and check our physical fitness. Thus I found myself completely naked standing at attention along with a column of men chosen for their apparent huskiness. Workers were needed for the coal mine at Jaworzno!

The army doctor checked us over carefully, listening to his stethoscope against our chests, feeling our biceps and peering inside our mouths. He pronounced a hundred of us in good enough shape for harder forced labor.

One sunny day soon thereafter we were loaded onto a truck and driven to a camp at Jaworzno, some six miles from Auschwitz. It was to be my last glimpse of the sun for some time. Right away we were sent down to the bottom of the mine, there to spend all our days except for Sunday, from six o'clock in the morning to six o'clock at night.

At that point the camp at Jaworzno was just being built. There were only a few wooden barracks, with one or two more beginning to rise. Jaworzno was one of the satellite camps around Auschwitz, being located there to meet the needs of a civilian company operating the mine. Similar camps existed at Monowitz and Miskowitz, where the convicts' living conditions stayed fairly standard.

At first glance, this camp had several advantages over Birkenau. It wasn't filthy, it didn't stink, it wasn't even very crowded. Its horizon wasn't spoiled by the grim outline of crematorium chimneys. Also, Jaworzno's installations, though primitive, were new; the three-decker bunks had fairly clean straw mattresses on them. And though the food was exactly the same fare that all convicts were given—the whole network's nutrition issued out of Auschwitz—it seemed to me that we got a little more to eat.

Furthermore, we neophyte coal miners looked forward to being under the orders of professional Meisters rather than the brutal kapos we knew; in the mines we'd be helping civilian work gangs. Considering the thousands upon thousands of Jewish, Russian, and Polish slaves draining swamps and building roads on the vast plains, we felt rather lucky. All in all, we congratulated ourselves on being raised to the status of miners.

We couldn't have been more mistaken! Work conditions turned out to be appalling. My team in particular had a very tough supervisor. We labored in stifling narrow galleries where it was hard to parry blows from the men with clubs (as sadistic as any we'd seen).

Those civilian German miners we'd looked forward to working with were not inclined to throw us any scraps from their meals, and seemed to find every incentive for exploiting us.

For interminable days on end I pushed coal-laden carts up those long, dimly lit corridors, beaten like a donkey en route. After the evening shower when the elevators had once more borne us to the surface, I could scarcely stay awake for the brown bread we were given for dinner.

The first month was painful, the second excruciating, and by the third a kind of mad desperation had set in.

We rose in the chill dawn at five o'clock and were given fifteen minutes to fall in for roll call. But what a roll call! Over and over we were counted, as there were always a few missing —some who'd been removed during the night, some who'd remained in their bunks incapable of stirring. Our captors were determined to know our exact number beyond the shadow of a doubt. They felt that prisoners would be most tempted to attempt escape here in this camp, so close to the outside where contact might be established with the civilian population.

Subsequently I cursed myself for not capitalizing on my presence at Jaworzno, though actually I'd have had to stay there longer to accomplish anything. True, at Jaworzno would-be resisters might have more opportunity to get together and organize, but their own mistrust stood in the way. It took time for a new prisoner to be accepted by a group fearful of informers.

Once our work party was assembled mornings, we wearily trudged the long road to the mine. The rough terrain would have made walking difficult even for well-fed men; what we'd received beforehand in the way of breakfast was some hot water! Yes, a bowl of water, just that and no more, served four people, and we counted every spoonful to make sure that it was equally divided. For it was absolutely all we got. Except for water our stomachs were empty all those morning hours that we toiled there without respite. In the intense heat of those galleries our raging thirst often drove us to drink our own urine. We all did. We would urinate into our cupped hands and then drink it. If by lucky chance a little trickle of water was found running down the rocks we would all rush to lick it.

At noon we were given soup, sometimes quite thick and made exclusively of boiled vegetables. We had a whole hour's midday rest period and we spent it looking for a little more food. Sometimes we were fortunate enough to nab a potato dropped from a civilian worker's lunch kit.

At one o'clock work resumed again for five more hours before we were hauled up to the surface. Then the exhausting long march back to camp. And the evening roll call, maddeningly repeated twice, thrice, or even ten times, after which we were given slices of black bread, which we tore apart like starving animals.

Never, never could we count on being able to rest. Often at night we had to work under spotlights, cleaning up the camp or doing construction work on it. Our masters gave us very little unbroken sleep. Whenever we closed our eyes it was with the knowledge that we might be waked in the still of the night to perform some task or merely to be counted again.

Although chores and roll calls were not waived on Sunday, it was still a day of rest and counted as a blessing—not that the day could possibly undo the week's damage to our bodies.

Our physical exhaustion was intensified by our chronic nervous anxiety and our permanent craven fear of being beaten. The hideous yowling commands of the kapos, their incessant barking of threats and vituperation, tore at our eardrums and pushed us even further toward collapse.

Every night I could see a tangible deterioration in my body. It became easier and easier for me to ring my thighs with my hands, and soon I could feel bone beneath the skin. Still, I could have held out a while longer except for my cruelly lacerated feet. Deep cuts under the toes, gashes which should have been sterilized and bandaged, had started to fester and mortify. But how to treat them? I didn't dare go to the infirmary because of its sinister reputation. Avoid it at all costs! dismissed patients always warned.

But at last came a morning—after a terrible nightmare-ridden sleep—when the hike to work seemed beyond me. My feet had swollen, and the right ankle was hideously painful to touch. Nonetheless, I managed to limp the whole two-mile march. Down in the mine shaft, as the dark day dragged on, I felt the blistering heat become a part of me. To gain a momentary rest I told the supervisor I had diarrhea, which was true in any case. Every hour I could feel my fever rising.

Every step back to camp was total anguish. My legs finally collapsed. Halting with the others in front of the barracks I had a sudden chill, my vision blurred, my knees buckled. They had to carry me to my bunk.

Willy-nilly, next morning it was the infirmary.

This dread place hardly merited the name of infirmary; no wonder prisoners had cautioned against it. One lone doctor and two or three nurses supposedly took care of all the ill lying untreated on their three-decker bunks (the same kind we had in the barracks).

The convict-doctor, who wore the same striped uniform as his patients, selected several of us from among the others, and he gave us a shot. What it consisted of, we knew not; rumor had it that some injections were lethal. But we were afraid to ask any questions—even if the doctor had spoken French. To me, he mumbled some phrase the only word of which I could catch was infection. All I knew was how fearfully my swollen ankles throbbed and ached; my comrades had complained of my keeping them awake the night before with my delirious moans and thrashing about.

I have no idea whether my shot was a cure or a sedative, but I had barely clambered onto the topmost bunk when I sank into a long deep sleep. When I finally awoke in the evening I was at least able to take note of my surroundings.

I was in a vast dormitory with a hundred or more beds stacked on top of each other. Almost all the beds were occupied by skeletonized beings whose deathly, hopeless appearance shocked me. I had seen plenty of Moslems before, but never so many all together like this. Besides, it suddenly struck me that I had become one of them, just another Moslem. All at once I felt that I had been condemned to death. I was very frightened.

Indeed, all of these sad gray creatures—impossible to think of them as men!—seemed to be stoically awaiting their ends. Most were quite fleshless though some were monstrously swollen; all were naked and hairless. Usually they expired during the night, their death rattles blending with the snoring of the others. In the morning, their bunkmates would request that the corpses be removed. This would be done when the work party got around to it.

That first evening I was sickeningly conscious of the stench. In the ward there was a perpetual and atrocious smell from fevered unwashed bodies, rotting flesh, soiled mattresses, and above all, the waste buckets—emptied occasionally by an orderly, or by two ambulatory patients whom he accompanied to the latrines.

We newcomers hadn't expected gaiety at Jaworzno, but we were appalled at the horror piled on horror. Never had I seen so much misery. In this foul atmosphere of rot and decay, it was all we could do to fight off despair.

To start with, the patients were not treated—but then how could they be? Aspirin and mercurochrome were the only supplies possessed by the tiny medical staff, who lived in a small room adjoining the infirmary. Except for that first morning's shots, I saw no other medication given. Obviously the Nazis figured that nature's cure was the best remedy. For a natural cure proved that the patient's body still contained a reservoir of strength and hence could still be used. Any need for medical attention revealed a lamentable weakness in the patient. Consequently the sensible thing was to let such expendable types die right away. Why prolong their frail lives with expensive medicines? And why raise any false hopes for this life? Certainly the Germans had no earthly reason to conserve human resources: human resources were what they had plenty of.

Under the terms of a contract signed between the Auschwitz S.S. and the manager of the Jaworzno mine a certain number of workers had to be provided every day. There was no requirement that they had to be the same workers, only that the exact number be forthcoming. So much human flesh had to be delivered, and on the hoof, so to speak.

To say that the Nazis let the patients die at the infirmary would be misleading. They actively speeded along the process. The real chief of the institution wasn't the unfortunate German physician who'd been sent to Auschwitz as an enemy of the regime, and who may have been a communist, a Jew, or a Freemason. He had no authority to speak of. The real head, a spruce, impeccably groomed army doctor, arrived at the "dream house" every morning to make a dashing entrance into the ward. He must have been the Oberarzt in charge of several infirmaries of the area.

At his dignified entry the nurse would shout out *Achtung!* and stand at stiff attention, while the doctor made his rounds. Made his rounds, but naturally enough treated no patients. This pompous figure was purely an administrator who usually only glanced perfunctorily at the papers handed him before giving instructions. We always watched him go with relief.

But from time to time he would select victims. With measured tread he would stroll between the rows of beds. Pausing to gaze dispassionately at particularly far gone cases, he would remove the man's chart from the bundle before proceeding. At the end of the ward he would count the charts, confer briefly with the other doctor, and then stroll out, dignity intact.

Half an hour later, just time enough to bring his register up to date and compile his lists, the orderly would appear to read out ten or fifteen serial numbers, explaining that their owners should get ready for evacuation to the Auschwitz Krankenbau. Everyone know what that meant, yet there wasn't a gasp, not a murmur. A few went off to weep silently in a corner, but most remained still and silent as if the news of their selection had been long expected and not unwelcome. No one was deceived. The Auschwitz hospital spelled death. They knew they would be taken immediately to the gas chambers. It was the same old story of room having to be made for the new crop of patients arriving daily at the infirmary.

Despite utter neglect my body began to repair itself. Gradually my foot healed and I grew in strength. For a week I remained there, eating more than usual; dying men's lack of appetite meant more food for the others. Of course a nourishing diet would have better restored my vigor, but the relative abundance of any food at all helped. My wounds healed amazingly quickly and the infection, along with the fever, went away too. Such cures in weakened bodies were quite rare, it seemed.

After only four days I could walk almost painlessly, and the orderly put me on latrine duty.

It's funny how you can adjust to anything. It's all in what you're used to. Conditions being what they were and with my knowledge of what awaited me when I went back to the mine, I'd have been perfectly willing to work in the latrine day and night to the end of the war, never mind the nauseating stench, the filth, and the depressing sight of death and decay all around me. I would have willingly continued to munch my black bread beside a bucket brimming with the excrement of patients unable to rise from their beds.

But all good things must come to an end. Try though I might, I couldn't think up any way to keep my soft job in the dream house, or to find another. The doctor said I must go back to work.

So with a heavy heart I returned to the mine. It was just the same—the two-mile march, the pushing and straining at carts in the suffocating gloom, and suffering torments from thirst. At this second stint I lacked all the energy I'd had before, and day by day I grew weaker. I tried to conserve my strength as much as possible, and to exploit any possible advantages there might be from being a veteran. Being an old-timer I knew a few people and was able to sneak a few favors and extra hunks of bread. But nonetheless I was going downhill fast.

One day, for no visible reason, I was sent on an errand to a factory under construction. Here I encountered an English prisoner working there as a mechanic. As chance would have it, at one point we found ourselves alone together, whereupon I immediately launched into an impassioned plea for his help in an escape attempt. For some time, consumed by thoughts of escape, I'd been ready for any kind of venture. To me this Englishman looked like a heaven-sent savior. He was a symbol of the Allied forces and a link with the outside world. Fervently I addressed him in every language I knew to convey my burning desire to escape and my urgent need of his help.

Unfortunately I didn't know a single word of English and that's all he spoke. And so, although this prisoner could see that I was a physical wreck, he did not share the hell that had made me so, and there was no communication between us. An insurmountable gulf separated us. As a prisoner of war and a worker he was not only protected by the laws of war but granted certain privileges. He hadn't the remotest idea what I wanted. He listened to me jabbering away for some moments, then smiled indulgently as if he had understood and brought out what he had in his pocket: half a package of cigarettes and a few chocolate bars.

My disappointment didn't prevent my speedy acceptance of this offer, for this unexpected bonanza could be bartered for several days of normal rations. Thus our frustrating encounter came to an end, it being difficult and seemingly pointless to extend. Later I tried to get a job that would allow me to see the Englishman again, but it was no use. Lightning never strikes twice in the same spot.

Back to the mines. And a few days later, despite all I could do, I landed in the infirmary.

This time my case seemed more serious. Once more my wounds gaped open, and once again my feet, ankles, and legs swelled angrily, far worse than before. Blood poisoning had set in. A soaring temperature made me barely conscious of what was going on around my bed. Four pus-ridden infections were lanced repeatedly, first by the doctor and then by the orderly, who must have been a rank amateur. I can still see this lout industriously gouging at my left leg with his scalpel. Yet perhaps his work prevented gangrene from killing me, for subsequently my fever fell, I grew stronger and began to take care of myself. The orderly brought me permanganate and paper bandages and I was able to chart my progress.

It seemed, though, that my high fever and inability to eat a morsel of food for so many days had wrought havoc in my appearance. The commiserating eyes of my neighbors showed me that I must look like a dying man ripe for the gas chamber.

And they were right. When the S.S. doctor arrived—"*Ach-tung!*"—I saw the well-known scene repeat itself. But this time I was chosen. First, however, I watched the cold-eyed officer in his spotless uniform stride about dispensing death up and down the aisles. His demeanor, no less than his role, was the antithesis of a life-giving physician. When he got to me he hardly glanced at my naked stretched-out body. One glimpse sufficed. He barely paused before picking up my chart and placing it in the orderly's hands. Now it was all over, I thought without emotion.

At the last bed he turned around and started counting the charts. I heard him pronounce the word *vierzehn*, fourteen. He seemed to hesitate for a moment as if wondering whether the figure was large enough. Then suddenly he disappeared.

I have no idea what went on in the next room where the orderly worked over his files. Minutes passed. My neighbor spoke to me in French across the aisle separating our bunks. Though his eyes still showed the aftereffects of fright he could relax now.

"They took your chart?" he asked.

"Yes."

"But that doesn't mean . . ."

He tried to comfort me, inventing all sorts of possibilities. I scarcely listened, bathed in a dull indifference. When the orderly reappeared he slowly read from the list he held. I waited to hear my own number: 130665, which I knew perfectly; German figures had become indelibly engraved on my brain.

But my number was not called, and the orderly had finished. Baffled, I sat up in bed. And I leaned across to my neighbor. "How many numbers did he call?"

"I counted thirteen."

None of them mine, yet my chart had disappeared! One of those never-to-be-explained mysteries, for I had no friends in the infirmary, and anyway no one would have dared try to save me. My chart had simply vanished through some freakish error such as the orderly's becoming momentarily distracted. I'd been saved by an invisible throw of the dice. Yet I couldn't really rejoice—I knew it was just a respite.

Sure enough, four days later the Oberarzt came back and unhesitatingly tabbed me. It was inevitable. The last four days hadn't supplanted any lost weight or improved my ghastly pallor. I still looked like a dying man.

This time the orderly came back with a longer list, and this time he read out my number quite clearly. I answered "present" and got up at once, determined to get it over without yielding to self-pity. I was fed up anyway with waiting and wondering and living in fear and quite ready to throw in the towel. Let them put an end to a life that hardly seemed worth living in any case. It was a pity to die at twenty-four, but then I could have been killed at the front like so many others.

I crawled into my shabby convict uniform and slapped the shapeless cap on my shaved head before joining the other chosen ones just outside the infirmary. There were about twenty of us human relics sitting on the ground in despondent attitudes as we awaited our last truck ride.

I looked at my feet in the clogs once more, and noticed that they were nearly cured. There were still scars where the scalpel had dug, but the swelling had receded and the skin looked healthy. And I could wriggle my toes normally. They had cured me only to kill me: a macabre joke I could dimly realize without appreciation. Most of my companions seemed equally phlegmatic. Three or four silently wept and one trembled convulsively with his mouth wide open as if he were stifling.

Finally the truck pulled up before us. We climbed aboard. Some of the condemned men had to be supported or pushed on. Not that any of them resisted or tried to escape. It was just that their numbed legs could barely walk.

At the rear of the truck two very young guards, with the S.S. insignia on their collars, sat leveling submachine guns at us. They chatted together companionably, with a good deal of chuckling. I knew enough German to understand what they were saying when they looked at us with such amusement. They were sincerely amused by our appearance—not particularly hostile or even insulting. They just gazed at us as if we were clowns in a circus. They knew perfectly well what awaited us, but it had no meaning. Perhaps they could have felt some emotion, either hate or pity, if they'd been taking flesh-and-blood men to be shot. But they obviously considered us broken-down robots, still-breathing carcasses who must now be disposed of.

For a fleeting moment I had an impulse to attack these callous men whose laughter grated, but I repressed it. I was too weak to hurt them and would only have been beaten for my pains. And I didn't need that extra suffering. The truck rolled along a straight deserted road across a sunny joyless landscape. Should I try jumping off the moving vehicle to die under a hail of machine-gun bullets? No, that wasn't the answer either.

Both soldiers were well under twenty, and I thought that to draft such youngsters Germany must be scraping the bottom of the barrel. As we had all known for some time, the Germans had suffered a string of defeats, the most serious being in Italy. Mussolini's fall from power, his capture and imprisonment by order of the king, and his replacement by Marshal Badoglio caused an enormous furor. The good news had even spread through the barbed wire to the camp a few days before, relayed to us by a new work team from Birkenau.

More important, we knew that the Allies had succeeded in landing in Sicily, thus acquiring an incalculable advantage. On the Russian front, thrusting Soviet armies advanced toward East Prussia, and in Tunisia the famous Afrika Korps neared collapse. Ironically, we prisoners were being liquidated just within sight of our armies' victory; perhaps we were only within a few days of being freed.

At last we were unloaded in front of the Krankenbau at Auschwitz. And there we waited some time. Inside we could see orderlies bustling about: we were certainly at the camp hospital, all right. Hope sprang uninvited, a small hope easily pushed down yet still glimmering at the realization that we might be weeded out a second time. We'd been so sure of going directly to our deaths, a final second selection had never occurred to us.

Yes, for some strange and mysterious reason the medical authorities at Auschwitz were to have their pick. And now it appeared that we weren't the only ones to be screened again; three other trucks drew up to unload their human cargoes so that there were now about fifty of us zombie-like creatures waiting in front of the hospital.

"Off with your clothes! Form a single file!"

An Oberarzt in a starched white tunic, his assistant, and the Schreibers. As the file of naked wraiths passed slowly before them, it was to be seen that this cursory examination resulted in another division. The doctor uttered one of two words for each man: either *links* or *rechts*. Very shortly the group on the left, *links*, began to swell and continue to do so. This was the death group.

Links, rechts, links . . .

At spaced intervals every few seconds the doctor's dry voice decided life or death. The Schreibers called out the serial numbers.

Links, links . . .

Inexorably the death group kept increasing, but not a sound, not a whisper, came from it. Now it was my turn. I stiffened. The seconds seemed endless.

"*Rechts.*"

Once again I had been saved.

8 AUSCHWITZ

I WAS SAVED, but for how long?

Everything depended on living conditions at Auschwitz. For after this medical examination, where my life hung by a thread, I was assigned to the main camp. The doomed group on the left, once again loaded onto the trucks, were driven outside the camp and we never found out any details of their end.

We few who escaped their fate went into the Auschwitz Krankenbau. The week I spent there was a real godsend to me, before having to resume hard work again.

Of the twenty-eight red brick barracks at Auschwitz, four made up the Krankenbau. It wasn't a proper sanitorium, of course. Patients lay on lumpy mattresses in three-decker bunks, three men to a bunk, and they still got the same awful rutabaga soup and hard black bread. They received no more medical care here than in the outlying infirmaries. And it goes without saying that we still underwent periodic thinnings of our crowded beds by the doctor.

Yet despite all that, this place was almost comfortable compared to the stinking hellhole of Jaworzno. Most amazing to us were the clean toilets in every barracks—a cleanliness unparalleled in our experience. The Auschwitz Krankenbau was blessedly free of the foul smell that reigned in other camps, and for this we were grateful.

The medical staff seemed more professional—not that one could exactly sing the praises of the indifferent doctor assigned to my case, who really had little to do with my recovery. But I was lucky enough to have an orderly who performed extra services for me despite his thousand other pressing duties. A few months later he was to provide me with still more valuable help.

It was he too who volunteered some rather interesting information. Until the beginning of 1943, Auschwitz had been under the direction of the Nazis' most ferocious killer. He had the prisoners, mostly Jewish, slaughtered in wholesale lots. After he left the situation eased a little; whether the new Lagerführer was actually less bloodthirsty or merely hoping to increase his charges' work capacity, in any case he adopted a more humane policy. He forbade all corporal punishment except for disciplinary measures, and he had a notice put up announcing that the inmates' lives would be spared if they did their work properly.

Theoretically these principles still obtained when I was transferred from Jaworzno to Auschwitz in November 1943. The situation was to remain stable for some time, a fact that doubtless explained the main camp's relatively good reputation among prisoners in satellite camps. I well knew the climate of terror in the nearest, Birkenau.

Sadly, the new principles remained mainly just principles, for there was no way of preventing even a kapo from just clobbering anyone he had a mind to, much less of challenging an S.S. officer's rights. Every convict knew what dire reprisals would descend on him if he made a complaint. Though we were struck at random less often, we were "punished" more, and nothing was easier than to find some pretext for punishment.

The primary characteristic to distinguish Auschwitz from its outlying camps was its thriving, many-faceted "organization"—

in the very special sense that the word assumed in concentration camp language. Since its very inception Auschwitz had been the headquarters for confiscating all the baggage of the deported prisoners and sending it by trainloads to warehouses in East Germany. This official looting had been going on for ten years.

That was why prisoners leaving Drancy were asked to bring along as many of their worldly goods as possible. Veritable fortunes accompanied the deported prisoners on those trains that brought them to camp—and there were two or three such trains daily at certain times of the year—as well as on those innumerable trains coming from Eastern Europe.

Gold, silver, rich clothing, diamonds, and other precious stones were all stacked in crates at Auschwitz warehouses. But the men in charge of classifying and sorting out these treasures were kapos, who in civilian life had usually been criminals. Naturally some of the swag stuck to their fingers, and they also set aside some for the S.S., since their tacit complicity had to be paid for. Every last one of them stole, traded, and waxed prosperous. And as all shared the guilt, none could denounce the others.

This made the camp relatively affluent—an affluence which attained dazzling heights in the case of the camp commanders, and gradually diminished till it touched the bottom of the scale. Its effects could still be seen at the level of the Haftlings or common prisoners, whom I now joined. With a little luck, some of the Haftlings could survive. At Auschwitz as at Mauthausen, at Buchenwald as at Nenengamme, the prisoners learned myriad ways and means to increase their diet.

I tried to hustle like the others, but without much success. You needed a lot of audacity and no scruples whatsoever. Occasionally I was able to sneak a slice of stolen bread, acquired more through stealth than through cunning. But most of the time I was reduced to squabbling with the others over the rotten vegetables filched from garbage cans.

Obviously, some craft was needed to assuage the gnawing

hunger that incessantly assaulted us all. An even harder requirement was that we must always be on guard. In this complex universe where all countries were represented, any member of a work team, or even a bunkmate, might reveal himself as an enemy. From the turncoat and traitor to the petty thief who snatched bread from under the very nose of his fellow slave, we had to keep a sharp lookout for every form of villainy. A moment's inattention could cause a man to be robbed blind, to miss out on a never-to-return opportunity, and even to find himself punished for somebody else's crime. I have seen many men falsely accused of helping in an escape attempt hanged along with the real culprits.

Useful contacts were a vital necessity and you had to do favors to expect any in return, know who to see and how to manage. For a start, you had to learn every language spoken in camp—German, Russian, Polish, Yiddish; eventually a combination of these four became the special dialect of Auschwitz.

Sooner or later we learned all the devious tricks to survival, just as they were learned by all the other prisoners in the camp's twenty-eight barracks. I learned which were the cushiest jobs and which the nastiest, which work groups to try for and which should be avoided like the plague. I learned to understand the kapos' mentality. I knew which kapos sadistically enjoyed inflicting pain on the prisoners; which were the lazy ones who shirked their duties and did as little as possible; which were vain enough to show leniency if you kowtowed to them and made a big show of respect. I fled from the sadists, worked like a demon for the lazy, flattered the vain with eager salutes, groveled before all.

You might think, with all that knowledge, that I managed to avoid punishment at Auschwitz. But I didn't. I received plenty of the *fünfundzwanzig auf Arsch*—the inevitable twenty-five lashes on the backside. Once I was caught loafing at the armaments factory, where I managed to work for a few months. Assigned to a group who reconditioned crates for munitions, I succeeded in repairing only two crates in two months. This piece of goldbricking stands out as my worthiest endeavor. We were supposed to repair an average of fifteen crates a day. With the complicity of a comrade in a responsible job, I would pile a stack of already repaired crates in front of me. Behind this rampart, which mutely testified to my industry, I would be seen zealously using my tools whenever the inspector passed by. Actually, my flying hands never left the one crate, which I assembled and dismantled incessantly.

But it was too good to last. One day a brighter than average S.S. checked my work and saw that I was cheating. Fortunately, he couldn't know how long the slowdown had been going on; two months' sabotage would have meant hanging. So he only condemned me to be whipped, and he himself took charge of the punishment.

I lowered my trousers and bent over the work bench. I was ordered to count the lashes aloud. *Eins, zwei, drei . . .* this kind of agony was already familiar to me. I'd gone through it at Chalon-sur-Saône at the hands of the Gestapo. I found that S.S. lashes at Auschwitz hurt as much as Gestapo lashes in Chalon, and the bullwhip equaled the iron ruler in pain. The difference was that now so much of my flesh had melted away. My chastiser's whip cut into muscles and skin that barely covered the unprotected bone. Each blow made my knees buckle. By the time he had finished I felt no pain. Half conscious, I vaguely heard the S.S. hurling one last invective my way and promising to have me strung up at the first opportunity.

And this was no idle threat. Many a time I'd been forced to stand at attention along with thousands of prisoners and made to watch hangings, invariably to musical accompaniment. The condemned men might be saboteurs, thieves who'd been caught red-handed, or failed runaways. We always knew the crime, for every man went to the gallows with a sign on his chest: I engaged in sabotage and I deserve death, I tried to escape, etc.

When I tried to straighten up again, my behind running with blood, I thought my lower back was paralyzed. For at least a week thereafter, I was unable either to sit down or to stand erect and could only attain the minimum of comfort lying on my stomach. Going to the latrine was indescribable torture, worse than the beating itself. But I was given a few days' rest, then transferred to another work team.

Auschwitz had its own women's camp, separated from us by a barbed wire fence. Sometimes we observed these miserable females, who were worked as hard, were fed as little, and died at the same rate as us. As I have said, somehow they looked even ghastlier than we did, from the distance that we saw them. Close contact was virtually impossible. Nevertheless, some of us had a chance to exchange a few words and once a female labor gang worked next to a male group. That was how we heard of the Allied troop landing in Normandy in June 1944. For reasons I never could fathom, the women at Auschwitz seemed to get all the news.

I have already spoken previously of their repulsive appearance, devoid of all femininity. Their bosses the female kapos looked as bad and behaved worse. I have seen them running along beside a column of women gleefully cracking their whips down on the defenseless backs. Yet we heard of a brand of females—the S.S. *Aufseherinnen*—who reached the epitome of cruelty and sadism.

Despite the fact that most prisoners had long since been drained of any sexual desire, some secret nighttime trysts did occur, at the price of extraordinary trickery, and were sometimes paid for with death. I was assured that for quite some time, naturally without asking for it, a few of the prisoners had received the favors of one of these female S.S. guards. One man in question, I think he was Polish, was protected by his mistress for months on end and given a soft job. I also heard that one German prisoner, a kapo in the women's camp, regularly gave herself to recently arrived young Haftlings.

The brothel available to S.S. guards and managers was built in 1943 and said to be quite luxurious. Kapos who happened to be in the good graces of the commander were occasionally allowed in too. They were given brothel tickets. One of our kapos loved to flaunt his brothel ticket with a gloating smile and many a lewd comment. Generally speaking, however, these brutes preferred to practice homosexuality, though it was theoretically forbidden.

The management and administrative organizations for the entire complex were located at the main camp at Auschwitz. In addition to the barracks which housed the prisoners, there were warehouses, kitchens, a special administrative and command building, plus four structures of the Krankenbau and lastly—in more ways than one—the mysterious "Block 11" where strange experiments on human guinea pigs were carried out. Even at the beginning we heard disturbing rumors of what transpired there—grisly operations which were performed mostly on women and which usually proved fatal. A few survived, however, to tell the tale.

I myself was to become acquainted with this famous Block 11, not to be hacked on by any knife-happy lab man but to be questioned. For this building also housed the Politische Abteilung, the Gestapo's political research department.

One of my roommates, a French-speaking Russian, told me of his hair-raising experience in the experimental biology sector which was run by the notorious Dr. Mendele. Along with about a dozen other selected persons he was ushered into a room on the first floor. After a long wait, toward evening they were simply put onto an operating table, tied down, and castrated without any anesthetic. The Russian didn't wait for his turn. As soon as he heard the first victim's screams he threw himself out the window, landing unhurt on the grass, and ran back to his barracks to hide. No one chased him. The others simply surrendered to the butchery with that incredible passivity that I had so often marveled at. They were never seen again. As for the Russian, he was sent to the gas chamber a few weeks later —not as punishment but simply because he had reached his limit of endurance and his illness condemned him to the scrap heap.

Because the high-ranking military chiefs were quartered in Auschwitz, the camp was inspected very often, with order and discipline literally a matter of life or death. We were watched like hawks all the time. The S.S. had made up their minds to train this motley herd of Jews, Russians, Poles, and gypsies to march with perfect military precision. To this end the rhythmic martial music always helped keep the marching workers in step en route to their jobs. There was absolutely no relaxation possible at Auschwitz. Awkwardness in military drill could be punished by death, though usually punishment consisted of a so-called sports session. Any number could play—depending upon the offense, an entire collectively guilty group or just one guilty, poorly coordinated individual.

The method they used was nothing out of the ordinary. It is common in every barracks all over the world. But in most barracks, it lasts only ten minutes and the exercisers are in robust health. At Auschwitz, gymnastics lasted an hour or more and often resulted in death. Men beyond a certain age would just expire of heart failure.

With a whole group of victims the sadistic brutes would vent their spleen on the clumsiest, and his misfortune gave a better chance to the others, whereas one lone man being punished ran a high risk of death.

One day I was given a private lesson. Marching into camp I had inadvertently lost step. The S.S. who was watching eagle-eyed from the guard post ordered me to break ranks and for an hour had me perform endless calisthenics at breakneck pace.

"Squat, stand, lie down, squat, stand, lie down, run . . ."

If any of my movements were incomplete or too slow, he would lash out at the offending arm or knee with his whip. It seemed my pounding heart would burst, yet I knew very well that he would kill me if I faltered.

But I got by. At Auschwitz, human endurance exceeded all imaginable limits.

9 POLITISCHE ABTEILUNG

IT happened in February 1944, during my fourth month at Auschwitz, when I had already outlasted most of the other deportees and was one of the rare survivors of the July 1943 convoys.

I was in the ranks during evening roll call, waiting for the end of the interminable name-checking, with which they deprived us of our rest, when an S.S. suddenly appeared. He had a paper in his hand and he called out:

"Haftling Kessel, 130665."

He beckoned. In a state of some alarm I left the ranks, worried as to what on earth they wanted me for. It was quite exceptional for them to address any prisoner by name; like all the others I'd been trained to answer to my number. What did this unusual summons mean? Not that there was any question of asking the S.S.

"Follow me."

I followed. I saw only the man's broad back under his black tunic as he calmly led the way. My head was in turmoil. As usual, apprehension and hope were mixed. Perhaps a special punishment for some error I'd committed at work? Long after the event one could still be punished for it.

On the other hand, maybe they were going to break the

news that I'd be released soon? Such absurd flights of fancy had a habit of infiltrating my thoughts despite my efforts to drive them away. I spent half my prison time stifling such wildly extravagant hopes. On this occasion they stemmed from last night's fragmentary and possibly completely fallacious gossip —Hitler was on his knees and about to surrender, secret peace negotiations and prisoner exchanges were going on.

Quite ridiculous, my present hope, but in that eventful period nothing seemed impossible, and it was so novel, so bizarre, to be called by one's own name! I had a queer sensation of again becoming my own self, of retrieving my personality and individuality.

We had arrived at Cell Block 11—the dread building where industrious physicians carried out grisly experiments. Here men and women were mere guinea pigs subjected to shots and amputations; stories of men castrated like sheep to become just as uncaring and phlegmatic sprang to mind.

Yet there was no time to wonder whether some bespectacled scientist was about to convert me into a eunuch as my guide ushered me into a rather large room on the first floor. Seated behind heavy wooden tables were four men in civilian attire. They reminded me of the policemen in Chalon-sur-Saône, and in fact they were the Auschwitz Gestapo, the Politische Abteilung.

The Political Department. Deportees were not entirely cut off from their past. There were files on those who'd been involved in politics or who had belonged to the Resistance. The purpose of this department was to keep a watchful eye on them, to ferret out and nip in the bud any secret associations that might be forming within the camps. It was often deemed necessary to conduct inquiries at the request of other departments in the police force, for the purpose of extracting information or confessions from prisoners.

It didn't take me long to get the picture. It immediately became apparent that various activities of mine that I'd presumed to be long and safely buried had now been exhumed.

Of course I had no idea how and why this belated inquisition had come about, and as a matter of fact I never was to know. Did my file filter through a whole labyrinth of bureaucratic channels before catching the eye of some curious police chief? Perhaps they had patiently waited for prison life to have weakened my resistance, sapped my morale. That hardly seemed likely since I could have died a hundred deaths before now. But maybe some new development had reopened the whole business; maybe a fellow Resistance worker had been arrested and given me away under torture. This wasn't completely impossible, but I prefer to believe that fresh Resistance activities in the Dijon area had led the police to reopen all the old files. For I was among them. It would have been standard procedure to get Kessel and find out what he knew.

The atmosphere was oppressive. Almost bare walls with only a picture of der Führer and the swastika, plus a few shelves holding books and files. For furniture, two massive tables, some straight-backed chairs.

Seated at the tables were four men smoking. The youngest, short and blond, was drinking a cup of steaming coffee whose fragrance drifted to me across the room. He seemed totally preoccupied with his coffee and played no part in the questioning until the end. The three others were shuffling papers, doubtless a transcript of my first interrogation and a report of the inquiry. These three were older, heavy-set, with unremarkable features. In fact their aspect was so ordinary that I'm quite unable to summon up a single physical feature of theirs. On the other hand, the countenance of the little blond policeman remains firmly etched in my memory.

The S.S. who brought me in announced, "Haftling Kessel," saluted, and then left.

Facing my enemies I felt very puny and helpless indeed. I had mechanically taken the cap off my shaven head before coming into the room and now stood at attention. With a casual glance at the miserable object before them the officials exchanged a little light banter concerning me, comments I understood readily enough, as much by their tone, gestures, and scornful inflection as by their words. Skepticism as to the importance of the business at hand, boredom with having to proceed with another probably fruitless inquiry, sarcastic sneers about the faraway powers that be who had ordered the inquiry; they spoke quite openly without the least concern as to my overhearing, and why should they? In human terms I was a cipher.

One of them motioned me to step forward and the questioning began. The man spoke fairly good French, though occasionally he had to fumble around for words:

"Your name's Kessel?"

"Yes."

"French?"

"Yes."

"Born in Paris, July 26, 1919?"

"Yes."

"You live at 72, rue Claude Descamps?"

"Yes."

"You were arrested in Dijon on July 14, 1942?"

"Yes."

"What were you doing in Dijon?"

So that was it. I'd have to adopt the same alibis and make my answers as convincing as before. I had become a fairly good actor in prison. I had learned how to cheat first of all in school, and then in the army, but I really perfected it at Auschwitz.

"I wanted to get across the demarcation line."

"No."

"I swear—"

"No!"

This last "no" was a bark, as only a Gestapo can bark; unfortunately the Gestapo bark was inevitably followed by bites.

"Are you trying to make a fool of me? Tell us what you were up to there, and be quick about it."

The hefty policemen stepped up on either side of me to

slap my face with their open palms. Tears of rage sprang to my eyes but I forced myself to continue lying calmly, swearing that I came directly from Paris and had been looking for someone to help me cross the line. I'd had money along to pay for this help, I maintained.

"Any baggage?"

"None."

Another slap which almost sent me reeling to the floor.

"Come on, let's have the truth. When you were picked up in Dijon you were not coming from Paris, you were coming from Chalon-sur-Saône. You were carrying arms."

"That's not true!"

"You're going to spill the beans, Kessel. You're going to tell us who you worked with. Because it's quite impossible for you to have been working alone and we know it!"

I continued to deny everything, but without really pleading. Held fast on both sides by the two brutes, I knew with awful certainty that I was going to get the most terrible going over of my life. However I behaved, the odds were that they would torture and kill me anyway. So why should I lower myself to crawl?

My interrogator must have sensed from my attitude that I was not about to back down from my story, so he adopted a different tack, an almost sweet reasonableness.

"Look, Kessel, I don't want to hurt you. But it's my job to find out everything you know. So much easier for you if you talk now! Because in the end, you must realize, you will talk. What we need to know is who gave you the arms and to whom you were bringing them. In return . . ."

He went on, carefully picking the right words:

"Now I can't promise to get you out of here, you understand perfectly well that's not possible, but what I can do is see that you get a soft job. We can always help people who are willing to cooperate. Right?"

The two who had grabbed me by the shoulders still held on, but they didn't seem to convey any particular hostility, perhaps because they had become bored by all the punishment they'd dealt out to past victims. They simply awaited the signal to go into action, while the little blond fellow with slicked-down hair didn't appear to be listening to the discussion.

I gritted my teeth. They could kill me if they wanted to, I would not speak, I would confess nothing. No problem. I determined to lock myself in obstinacy, hold out for oblivion. I would seek unconsciousness.

Given a severe enough battering, I knew this could be done.

The beating didn't start right away. For a while the policeman continued haranguing me in his halting French, so near that I could smell his foul tobacco breath as he offered various bribes in return for my cooperation. He said that he would put in a good word for me to the *Obersturmführer*, the camp commander.

Actually, he didn't put much conviction into this, perhaps because he doubted whether I really knew anything as charged or, more likely, because he had become accustomed to failure. Certainly he must have known that I put no faith in his promises. Once I admitted to membership in a Resistance network I was as good as dead. I rather doubt whether the officials of the *Politische Abteilung* obtained many confessions in the concentration camps.

While giving me time to reconsider he chatted in German with his colleagues and lit a cigarette.

"Do you want a smoke?"

"No."

Recess ended, he went over the same ground again, and with the same results. Then he sighed:

"Too bad for you!"

With that the two thugs went into action. It was the standard two-man shellacking. I had endured it more than once. The tormentors pummeled their victim from one to the other, and in a few minutes I was hammered black and blue, my nose bleeding, my ears a mess. I couldn't keep from crying out. But mercifully each blow on my head dimmed my awareness a little.

Staggering, I tried, vainly, to protect my face and especially not to fall; once on the floor many prisoners were kicked to death.

At last they stopped for a moment to ask me once more to talk. I still maintained I didn't know anything.

A new beating. This time they had no trouble knocking me down: soon I was on the floor, rolled up in a ball to protect my belly, only half conscious and my face swollen and bloody.

Then suddenly they left me alone there while I heaved and panted for breath. Apparently the four men had lost interest in me; they chatted amongst themselves about camp affairs. For a moment I had a mad hope that they would let it go at that, that I had succeeded in convincing them and that they were about to end the interview with a simple kick out the door.

But no, now they dragged me out and methodically started the same process over again. They knew their business, all right. They cleverly found the spots that would hurt excruciatingly without knocking me out. They hoped that in the long run I would cry for mercy.

Finally they hauled me over to the tables and pushed me into a chair. They were patient men in no hurry, and time was working against me. Each moment's respite helped lower my resistance by arousing new pain, letting fear invade my consciousness and dim my will power.

They sat down facing me and now I began to tremble convulsively as the short fair man who had said nothing began to open up a medical kit in his lap. With finicky deliberation he took out pliers and scalpels of various sizes. Looking at me at the same time, he smiled gently as if he were setting up a game. He toyed with his chrome-plated instruments, hesitating before making a choice.

Slight, blue-eyed, well-groomed, he didn't look brutish; he seemed almost delicate in his movements. Finally he took a small pair of pliers, picked up my left hand and applied the instrument to the nail of my middle finger, driving one tong of the tool under the nail to get a better grip. Then he pulled.

I screamed. He paused for an instant, smiling all the while, then pulled again. I watched the nail come out slowly, millimeter by millimeter. He never stopped smiling, holding my own pain-racked paw in a vise-like grip. His grip was inexorable despite my writhing and screams.

Finally he let me go. I stopped screaming but could not stop the jagged sobs as I looked at my torn hand.

"Well, Kessel, had enough?"

It was my old interrogator who spoke. He stood up, the better to inspect his colleague's work, then sat down ponderously, like a man with all the time in the world.

"Now then. Who gave you all those revolvers?"

This time I'd had it. I was on the point of giving in. If I could only make a dash for it, jump out the window as my colleague had done to keep from being castrated! But they surrounded me and the window was closed.

There was only one thing left to do—confess, as they were relentlessly forcing me to. Now I had to battle with myself, and it took all my strength to resist the temptation to speak, simply speak and tell them where I had uncovered the arms. Anything if they would only leave me alone!

Yet despite the atrocious pain clouding my thoughts, I knew that I could not get out of this so simply, that confessing where I had found the arms would not be enough to satisfy them. That would merely whet their appetite for more confessions to be extracted from me, before they finally put an end to me.

At all cost I mustn't give in, must hold out somehow . . .

I have trouble putting a clear sequence to what happened after that because I continually lost consciousness, regained it only to lose it again. Through a mist of agony I seemed to feel a scalpel digging into my flesh, loosening my finger at the base. An eternity of that.

When they slapped me back into final consciousness I threw

up. It was like a ghastly dream, yet I clearly remember a large, shiny pair of pliers which took the dangling bloody finger and tore it out with a twisting motion.

"That's all, Kessel!"

Half fainting I stumbled toward the door doubled up with pain, dripping blood and nursing my mutilated hand. I don't remember getting down the stairs. Perhaps some orderly accompanied me to the infirmary. I only remember that it was very cold and that the ground was covered with a thin layer of snow.

I spent three days in the infirmary, looked after by the French nurse who had taken care of me before. He put some permanganate powder on my wound and bandaged it with a strip of paper. Pain, shock, and nervous exhaustion made rest impossible the first night. Although my face was swollen from the beating and my body covered with bruises, all my powers of sensation concentrated in my poor hand, and all my capacity to suffer lay there. It seemed to me that I would never be able to use it again.

On the first morning a prison doctor making his rounds took a cursory look at my hand and then passed on without a word. The nurse came back once to change the wrapping. And after that, I took care of it as best I could, dusting it with the powder. Achingly I would clamber down from my bed to stagger off in search of my nurse, who would secretly supply me with the antiseptic.

All the time I knew this couldn't go on for very long, that they would only leave me there until the next ovenload was ready. It wasn't necessary to pick me out, the decision had already been made at a higher echelon.

And sure enough, during the afternoon of the third day as I lay with closed eyes trying to sleep, I heard my name bawled out in German.

"Kessel! 'Raus! Schnell!" Up and out!

Numbly I managed to get outside, to find myself joining a crowd of abject prisoners assembled in front of the Krankenbau. They were awaiting orders to start walking. Their last march, and they knew it: their faces were pale, set in despair. Quiet and orderly, though. There were about two hundred of us.

"Antreten!"

But we still had to dress up in ranks, correctly aligned.

Five in a row, and marching in step. S.S. guards with whips walked briskly beside the column, lashing out at those who lagged behind. And the stragglers summoned up their last strength and even ran so as not to perish there all by themselves, so as to go to their death with the others.

"Links, links!"

The last march. Dumb submission or fatalistic resignation, only a few could be heard whimpering. I too was completely resigned, plodding forward like an automaton. I didn't even speculate as to how we were going to be executed. What was the point? I had succeeded in postponing the inevitable until now, but it was bound to happen sooner or later. After all, it had been coming for a long time.

One, two. We approached the area of the crematorium with its billowing black clouds of smoke. A light wind fitfully blew the smoke across the gray sky.

Here they had us halt to wait along the wall.

Another column of prisoners arrived from another direction. Like us they were due to die. Where had they come from? Probably from an outside camp, and yet the authorities hadn't even taken the trouble to give them the customary final medical examination.

More came, a third column. Undoubtedly our bunch had to wait for enough others to assemble to fill a gas chamber. At least that's what I assumed later; at the time we had heard only very vague rumors as to how the mass executions were carried out.

Now we were ordered to take off our clothes and lay them neatly folded along the wall. We did so. There we skeletons stood barefoot in the snow, the cold penetrating to the very marrow. Shivering, we kept waiting until some S.S. roared up on motorcycles. They stopped and jumped off, it seemed to reinforce the other soldiers. One of them, a noncom, took up a position only a few meters away.

I glanced at him mechanically simply because he was there. Soon, however, I began to focus in on him. It wasn't his individual face that I recognized—probably I'd never seen him before in my life. But there was something that I did discern immediately, the marks of a boxer: broken nose, ridges over the eyes, cauliflower ears.

Unmistakable. The stigmata of the ring. He also had muscular shoulders and a springy way of walking. I hesitated for a second and then thought, oh, what the hell!

Naked and shivering I walked up to him. I don't know if it was a dim hope behind my overture, or some irrational kinship felt by boxers the world over, across all boundaries. I simply blurted out in German:

"Boxer?"

"Boxer? Ja!"

He didn't wait for me to explain, he understood. I too had a broken nose. An enormous bond existed between the two of us, despite the poles-apart difference in our positions. A few feet away, naked scarecrows stared at us and forgot for a moment their imminent deaths.

He questioned me.

"Where'd you fight?"

"Pacra, Central, Delbor, Japy, and once at the Vel d'Hiver."

Focal points of boxing, universally known. Something like a smile flickered briefly over his flattened face, revealing a row of metal-capped teeth. He hesitated for a moment, looked around, and made a quick decision.

"Get on!" he bellowed.

Apparently he was in charge of the S.S. detachment; I suppose he didn't stand to lose a thing. Anyway, the miracle had happened. He readied the motorcycle and started up the engines, with a casual wave at the back seat. I could scarcely believe my eyes.

I made a motion to get my clothes back, but he repeated the shout:

"Get on!"

Just as I was, bare as the day I was born, I climbed on behind him and clung to the saddle for dear life. As we started off, I could hear the whistle for assembly.

Once again I'd been saved! This broken-nosed S.S. man who had plucked me from the door of the gas chamber now drove me straight to the Krankenbau. It must have been a weird and unforgettable sight, the pathetic nude prisoner riding behind an S.S. on the back seat of a motorcycle, running right through the center of Auschwitz. And in this unusual posture, the bare prisoner prattling away to the Nazi, rambling on about his class and weight in the ring, the names of his trainers and other fighters, and all this in a rather hit-or-miss type of German.

I never saw him again. Being attached to the execution squads, he lived in a world apart, utterly cut off from mine. This act of mercy which he had performed in the name of boxing meant something totally different to each of us. Obviously to me it was everything; for him, nothing at all. I was like a worm that one doesn't step on at the last minute, a scrap of wood saved from among a thousand other scraps being tossed into the fire, saved for no good reason.

In addition to the mass executions to which he was a party he must have been individually responsible for scores of other murders. He was a professional killer, a former boxer who knew how to strike in S.S. style. He saved me without a moment's reflection, or if he did reflect it was assuredly to realize that I was due to die whatever happened, and that his gesture would only grant me a brief reprieve.

In any case he completed the gesture. Not only did he save me from the crematorium, he undoubtedly recommended me to someone in the Krankenbau, where I was officially listed as returning and kept until my wound had completely healed. Ten days. That was enough to put me back in shape.

I had no further contacts with the Politische Abteilung. I imagine they pigeonholed the file, having digested the report on their last inquiry. No one seemed concerned about whether Haftling Kessel had been gassed or not.

Again he was merely one of the shifting mass of twenty-five thousand prisoners. Anonymous in a new striped uniform, Haftling Kessel had become a number again, the only difference being that he was missing a finger from his left hand.

10 ESCAPE

Subsequently I served a full year in Auschwitz, no mean feat in itself. My knowledge of the camp, its organization, resources, and customs; my natural sturdy optimism; the friendships that had been made with some of the older prisoners—all these factors enabled me to hang on, come what may, throughout the year 1944.

My inherent optimism—which owed a lot to my fighting nature and active temperament—gradually was reinforced by a conviction that I would eventually be saved, that I was not to die at Auschwitz. Since my miraculous rescue by the broken-nosed former boxer, each day that I lived through seemed a sort of bonanza that fate had thrown my way and which it could not validly take back. Having survived blows, torture, illness, and several death sentences, I had acquired a fatalistic outlook, a calm certainty that I had a right to live out a normal life span. Such superstitious feelings came to the fore easily in a concentration camp. This particular feeling helped to keep me alive, and to a large extent spared me the dejection that burdened most of the prisoners and hastened their end. Confident of eventual survival, I was able to take events as they came without undue worry and dread ahead of time, and this was surely the best way of getting through them. I quickly became aware that a daring, devil-may-care attitude paid off, for, however one behaved, the punishment fell indiscriminately upon us all; there was no escape from it simply by working extra hard, obeying with alacrity, or slavishly following orders. Instead you had to cheat brazenly, lie without a second's hesitation, and make the most of every chance. By following this code I managed to scrape through even the nastiest jobs and cope with the most murderous kapos without getting killed.

Not that my shenanigans earned me any actual protection, or any soft job: I had my share of all the peril and all the various afflictions. Like everyone else I suffered from diarrhea, was eaten by open sores and wounds and reduced to the state of a skeleton. My mutilated hand made working all the more painful. Venomous hatred and cruel punishment were inevitable and I knew them well. But my belief in survival gave me the courage to hang on.

There was still another factor that boosted the morale of those who, like me, had made it through to 1944: the cheering certainty that Germany would be defeated. In spite of all our masters' efforts to the contrary, news still reached us; they could not keep us utterly sealed off or prevent our having some contacts with the civilian population. Some commandos working in the mines or armament factories got information from German and Polish civilians and brought it back to the central camp. The Krankenbau was a real news center.

So as early as that spring we knew that decisive events were in the air. Morale definitely improved. And in June came word of the fall of Rome and the massing of the Allied armies. In July, we heard tantalizingly brief and distorted rumors of the attempt on Hitler's life. Of course, we did not immediately grasp the shattering significance of this event, as official propaganda had very much minimized the extent of the military conspiracy. Nevertheless, it was enough to know that German officers had been sent to the Auschwitz area, and that many of them had been executed and burned in the crematoriums. Our crematoriums! True or false, this report aroused wildly extravagant hopes. Furthermore, the local civilians felt confident that the Russians were drawing near. The vise was closing on the conquered territories to the east, which were not far from us, and air raids on the industrial installations of our area exposed proof of Germany's weakened ability to resist. We were aware too that terrible bombing raids were devastating all of Germany, making a lie of Göring's boastful speeches. And finally in August came the Allied landing in Provence!

All this made me feverishly impatient. It is always hard to have to work for the enemy under any circumstances, but perhaps the most galling are when you know that the enemy is vanquished. I had never really given up hope of escaping and now it seemed to be not only the best solution but almost a duty. Nowadays I was ever on the lookout for the means, or any kind of chance. But the trusted few that I confided in—few because informers were a constant danger—considered me crazy. There were too many hazards. Barbed wire, watchtowers, the S.S., informers, fierce hunting dogs trained to smell out fugitives and track them down, a hostile countryside, the civilian population which was either terrorized or indifferent, the problem of hiding and obtaining clothes and food—all these factors, to say nothing of our wretched physical condition, pointed against any escape attempt.

Even the most reckless of my pals considered an escape quite impossible, as a relentless propaganda within the camp kept drilling into us. Besides the S.S. and kapos, posters everywhere proclaimed: "It is absolutely impossible to escape from Auschwitz"; there were also periodic hangings as well as informal dispatches via a bullet in the back of the head, for those rash souls who had tried to escape. Undoubtedly there had been runaways, but these were sudden impulses, bursts of mad despair rather than deliberately prepared attempts. Invariably runaways were caught, and after being shot in Prison Block 10, the bunker, their bodies were allowed to swing from the gibbet for three days. Much of the credit for the capture went to the dogs, fearsome, ferocious, perfectly trained beasts whose sense of smell seemed infallible.

Either just for fun, or perhaps in order to maintain their

conditioned reflexes, the S.S. frequently loosed the dogs upon us during roll calls, urging them to snap at any arm or leg that moved. It was too bad for anyone who twitched; you had to stand there like a statue and let yourself be mauled. The dogs would only let go when ordered to do so, leaving the marks of their fangs in our scrawny bodies.

We knew how quickly these animals could catch up with any runaway who didn't have at least a day's head start or friends on the outside. In any case, a successful escape was not a matter of crossing the frontier to freedom; the best one could hope for would be to join the bands of Polish partisans living and dying in the distant forests.

Such considerations didn't deter me. I wouldn't have hesitated an instant for the chance to fight with the Resistance, be it for years on end if need be. As the months dragged by, my nervous impatience grew, so that at times I found myself weeping from sheer frustration. At this period I would even have jumped at an opportunity to set out alone, having been unable to find anyone willing to join me.

But finally, quite by chance, I found what I was seeking in my own work gang.

One day I happened to overhear a whispered furtive conversation between two Poles who were part of my work group. They hadn't seen me, and the place was such that I was hidden from them. I knew a few words of Polish, which I had picked up here and there; as I remarked earlier, a hodge-podge of mixed languages had developed at Auschwitz. A combination of Slavic and German enabled the prisoners to understand each other, at least in the mundane business of our existence. The word for "escape" was part of this language, and my ears pricked up at the sound of it.

From then on I began a careful watch of the two men with all the patience I could muster and creating every possible opportunity to be near them. It didn't take me long to discover that they were part of a secret little band.

At last I decided the moment had come to reveal my intentions; I took aside one of the plotters, the one who seemed youngest, and flatly informed him that I intended escaping with him and his group. He pretended to be amazed, utterly astounded, and denied knowing what I was talking about. I insisted; he turned his back on me and swore. Later on I was to discover that he had learned a little French when he'd worked as a miner in northern France, but on this occasion he wouldn't admit to understanding a word of French and pretended that he couldn't make head nor tail of my gibberish. Although it seemed likely that I might be dealing with a hard core of political militants, possibly communists, the language that we used was too limited for us to be able to exchange any ideas on the subject. Anyway, at this period my political training was rudimentary, nor did I think it necessary to select friends and associates on the basis of their political opinions. The Poles, however, did think so. But even if I had been a communist and known as such, the fact that I was French made them distrust me. A barrier separated all nationalities.

The following day I stubbornly returned to the topic of escape—with the same spectacular lack of success. Once again, the man simply began swearing at me. And God knows Polish swearwords can be obscene. He covered me with the vilest insults. He irritated me, and in turn I resorted to the only method left to me: blackmail. I threatened to denounce him and his friends unless they let me join them. In actual fact, I hadn't the least intention of doing so; and in any case it was well known that informers (even potential ones) often ended up strangled under their beds. Yet I saw no other way to convert this man. Perhaps the method was a little underhanded, but I was devoured by impatience and would have stopped at nothing.

This time he blanched visibly, his consternation an admission in itself. He stalled, saying he must consult his friends, he had no say-so himself, and he would let me know what they jointly decided.

I knew that there were four of them, and I imagine that

they made some discreet inquiries about me. Had the information seemed unfavorable they could just have easily killed me —I was in danger even before the project got under way!

I waited a few days, got bored with waiting, and again tackled the young Pole. He told me that we'd have to wait a while longer, that the plan wasn't quite perfected in its details and that he would alert me when the time was ripe. The idea that they might take off without me drove me mad, but there wasn't a thing I could do. But, little by little, their mistrust melted; I knew that I'd been accepted when one of the men began using a few French phrases.

At last, one night in November 1944, I was summoned after roll call to a secret meeting around the corner of the prison block. All four men awaited me. One was ordered to withdraw, to stand watch. Then they announced that they had decided to take me along though with grave misgivings. What they feared most, they said, was not treachery but weakness. I wouldn't deliberately denounce them, they felt, but I might get nervous, panic, lose heart at the last moment and blunder in such a way as to wreck the whole enterprise. If that happened, they vowed with conviction, they would certainly kill me.

All this was conveyed not only in words but in the primitive sign language they used as supplement. And I hadn't the slightest doubt about the genuineness of the death threat; the four of them would be perfectly capable of carrying it out. Using the same language, I did my utmost to impress them with my resolution.

Now we were one. Our chief spokesman and obvious boss was a Pole about forty-five years old whom I'd noticed in the factory where we worked without realizing his major role in our adventure. He was a calm-appearing, conscientious, and silent worker; I knew him to be cool-headed and energetic, with long experience in underground activities. Now he let me in on the plan.

When I look back on it, I realize that the plan was sound

and the strategy could have succeeded despite its apparent idiocy. It called for boldly leaving the work site in the broad light of day. After a six-hour walk, we would reach temporary haven—an isolated house where one of our group had a relative. We would of course be expected, and from this point on, a chain of trusted accomplices would lead us out of the danger zone.

Obviously the whole plot hinged on this fortuitous relationship; without it no escape was possible. The carefully forged link with the outside world had been established thanks to sympathetic civilian factory workers.

Auschwitz Poles, notably better united than the other prisoners, also had the advantage of close proximity to a population whose support they could count on. And our leaving the work site by day could also be justified. For although a nighttime escape might at first seem to be more convenient, it would actually be impossible due to the many roadblocks. Furthermore, I had never heard of a successful escape attempt at night through the barbed wire which surrounded the camps. To leave from the work site, on the other hand, was relatively simple: the problem consisted in walking off quietly without attracting attention, yet fast enough to win in the pursuit which would inevitably follow. Everything depended on the head start we had achieved when the alarm was finally given.

Four days later, in the early morning, we were to stage our attempt.

We had agreed to meet at the Holzplatz—the work site where they unloaded wood—on a signal given by our leader. We had been assigned to two different parties working in a munitions factory about fifteen hundred yards from Auschwitz.

At about eight o'clock that morning came the signal. I had a legitimate pretext to leave my workbench—dysentery, and with it a built-in reason for hurry. The kapo I worked under gave me permission to leave, but told me to make it snappy. I knew that he had several crews to watch over, that he was permanently stationed at the other end of the shop, and that it wouldn't be too easy for him to notice that I had really disappeared.

We plotters were to meet at a chosen point on the vast area crisscrossed by trucks loaded with equipment and crews of laborers. A Bausten guarded the area. Obviously he could not watch everything at once, even though he was in the best position to do so.

My four Poles arrived at the rendezvous within seconds of each other, carrying picks and shovels. We had noticed a wheelbarrow in which sand was carted occasionally. One of the Poles grabbed the wheelbarrow handles and the rest of us followed, our tools slung over our shoulders. To the bored sentinel who watched us pass, nothing distinguished us from any other work crew. Furthermore, there was quite a crowd milling about, over three hundred workers occupied at various tasks. Some loaded trucks, some unloaded them, others pushed carts, dug or leveled earth, and always at the hustling pace forced upon them by the kapos and under the usual clouts and bellowed abuse. No reason for the guard to take any special notice of us.

Silently we threaded our way through the mass of prisoners, all wearing uniforms identical to our own. Now it was a matter of making our getaway onto the road, which was the sole access to the factory. If we could only make it through without being called! An enormous pile of garbage and debris filled one end of the Holzplatz. Often, at mealtime, the hungriest prisoners would pick and scavenge there, hoping for an edible morsel.

One of the Poles circled round the pile of refuse with his wheelbarrow, while another climbed up and pretended to shovel the waste, waiting until the S.S. turned his back before sliding down on the other side. One by one, we followed his example.

We had succeeded! Now we were outside the work area, steeling ourselves to make steady progress without running. Running would attract attention and also tire us out prematurely. We walked along the road at a regular even pace, without a glance to left or right.

On the right was a well-maintained road. The weather was cool and damp, the soil wet from the previous night's rain. The sky was overcast. We knew that less than four miles away we must quit the road to cross open fields, after having abandoned the wheelbarrow. Now we must proceed as quickly as possible toward a point which my companions knew, but I didn't.

We pressed on across the first few yards. No one had paid us the slightest attention. If our comrades had noticed our leave-taking, they hadn't given us away. Maybe they hadn't even speculated about our departure, for after all we could easily have received an order to do some job. Only our crew foremen might have noticed that they were missing a few men, but even in this event they wouldn't immediately think of an escape—it didn't happen often enough.

Once we felt that we were out of sight we began to put on speed. To save breath, none of us spoke. In our pockets we carried a few pieces of stale bread, saved over the preceding days, and which we now munched on as we hurried along.

We reached a curve in the road, gently encircling a little hill. This was the crucial point where we must desert the road and forge ahead into the fields. Straight on, a hundred meters or so, was an old dilapidated farm building. Perhaps it had been abandoned or evacuated by order of the German authorities. A desolate scene, without a single peasant in sight. Hiding the wheelbarrow in the field we set off separately, our clogs sticking in the wet earth.

Visibility was low due to the overcast and drizzle, and this reassured us a bit. From the tall watchtowers of Auschwitz it might perhaps have been possible with field glasses to make out five prisoners in striped uniforms edging forward slowly, single file, across the immense open fields, but apparently the alarm had not been sounded.

Panting, we rounded the hill and found to our dismay that

the road paralleled us at about three hundred yards or so. This spelled danger, as on this road every truck or car carried enemies. All we could do, whenever we heard the buzz of an engine, was to fling ourselves onto the ground, flattened and motionless in an attempt to blend in with the earth. Even the tiniest movement might attract someone's eye. We had to wait tensely, our noses in the furrows, unstirring until the vehicle disappeared over the horizon and we dared resume walking again.

In certain spots, we felt so glaringly visible that we dropped down to crawl. After a while we were exhausted and, despite the cold, soaked in sweat. It was vitally important to avoid all flat ground wherever we could, to run in the furrows Indian file, to seek shelter from the few trees whenever possible. We had to put all our trust in our leader, who, advancing ahead, could see the terrain.

Around ten o'clock a detachment of motorcycles roared onto the road. From a great distance we had heard the ever louder din of their engines. We had no saving protection—neither trees nor unevenness of terrain, and despite the distance the motorcyclists had only to look in order to see us as easily as we could see them. We threw ourselves onto the ground, as immobile as rocks. I suppose that the others were like me, sick with anxiety. I could see the man closest to me soundlessly moving his lips as if he were talking to himself; perhaps he was praying.

The cyclists sped by, the sound of their engines dying away. It was not a patrol out looking for us. At least nothing seemed to indicate it.

We kept on going.

It was about eleven o'clock when we heard the first howl of the sirens. We started trembling again. If it were only an air raid alert then nothing could be better! Our keepers would be too busy trying to find shelter from the bombs to look for us. But it might be the alert signaling an escape.

With no way to ascertain the cause of the sirens, we lunged

forward, running until we were staggering from fatigue. We had already come a long way from Auschwitz, over a distance difficult to estimate but probably more than four miles. Unfortunately our pursuers had cars and they must have a shrewd idea which direction we had taken. Furthermore, the area to be searched was not unlimited. Instinctively we veered away from the road toward a clump of trees on the left that we thought would hide us. On the way to it, a new detachment of motorcyclists whizzed down the road and once more we flattened out on the ground. As a matter of cautious policy we crawled to the woods and dove through to the blessed trees.

Now we held a desperate council of war, we five prisoners sitting on the aromatic leaves of the underbrush, dripping with sweat and chilled by the rising wind, our uniforms soggy with wet earth.

Our leader thought for a moment before he had his say. He was, if possible, even more anxious than the rest of us because he had the responsibility of decision. He proposed that we should spend the day in the deepest part of the forest so that we could start off again at nightfall, when our pursuers would have had a full day's unsuccessful search and when darkness would help our advance with a minimum of risk.

Someone else spoke up to disagree: he considered this a dangerous tactic, for we would be caught in a trap. The dogs would soon find our tracks, he said, and even if we did succeed in covering them, the hunters could still comb the relatively small, well-defined area to be searched. He argued that it would be best to scatter—to separate from each other and take off immediately, staying as far apart as possible. Hopefully the dogs might concentrate on the same track, and this way not everyone would be caught.

This seemed sound thinking, but for purely selfish reasons the plan didn't suit me at all. Its adoption meant that I would be the red herring who was sacrificed. I didn't know the country at all, or how to reach the intended hiding place. Therefore I spoke up against the plan, even though I felt pessimistically certain that my opposition would be in vain. Had my Polish friends decided that it was in their interest to abandon me, I was sure, they would do so without the slightest qualm.

Much to my surprise, though, they finally settled on the first plan—not because of any compunction about sacrificing me but because everyone was loath to be alone. Besides this instinctive feeling, there was our utter exhaustion, accentuated by hunger, cold, and thirst. We simply lacked the stamina to strike out in a new direction even though the Poles knew the region and assured us that our goal awaited us only a couple of hours away.

In our present feeble condition, a two-hour trek over open enemy territory, every inch fraught with danger, was just too much. Wretchedly we collapsed on the wet ground.

An hour passed. None of us said a single word to each other. What was the use! Everything was out of our hands now. If I had been a believer I would have prayed.

A fine misty rain began to fall which froze us still further. In the drizzle we huddled together and put our arms around each other for warmth, the old misery reflex of the camps, where unhappy bodies latched together hoping to be less miserable. Dreamily I began to concentrate on my family, on my older brother, who had been killed at Zuydecoote, on the younger, a prisoner of war, and on my parents . . .

I knew that Paris had been liberated three months before, and the thought of Paris obsessed me. My thoughts kept returning to Paris; I wondered if I'd ever see it again.

It was about two o'clock that afternoon when we heard the faint distant sound of an engine. It would stop, then resume again.

One of the Poles got up and climbed a tree in order to scan the horizon. We waited anxiously, our hearts in our mouths. We clung to the desperate hope that the sound meant nothing at all, merely the usual trucks rolling along the road to Auschwitz.

The man quickly shinnied down. I could see the staring

frightened eyes in his bony face. He muttered in his own language, but there was no necessity to translate. He had seen motorcycles circling slowly and stopping. There could be no doubt about it. It was not a convoy of trucks, it was a patrol.

Blind panic, a common unreasoning terror, drove us all to our feet to dash ahead. Exhausted as we were, we ran pell-mell through the forest without thought of where we were going, but very soon our heedless flight halted. Less than thirty yards away yawned another open space and we could not ignore the fact.

Utterly demoralized, drained, we abjectly returned to our original position and huddled there, incapable of making any decision, incapable of any thought at all.

Soon the noise started up again as if the patrol were getting closer. I never knew exactly what our pursuers did to find us or how long the hunt had lasted. I never even knew how our flight had been discovered. Maybe the S.S. had begun to look for us long before they gave the alarm. In any case, I'm not even sure that the sirens we heard were the alarm.

The way we knew that our capture was inevitable was the barking of the dogs. At first they were so far away that we could barely hear them—low hoarse barks of dogs at work, rising from time to time. Then louder baying as they became excited. After which, for a long suspenseful moment, they seemed to stop and the yammering died away. This was our last false hope. All too soon they started up again, increasing in volume as they got closer and closer.

We sat there paralyzed until they were almost upon us. In a last burst of despair we jumped up, determined to sell our lives dear. Desperately we grabbed the branches around us in order to make some sort of weapon. Of course we would be machine-gunned down at close range by the soldiers, but perhaps we'd have the chance to take just one S.S. with us before we went down.

It was the dogs, though, that surged forward, in a cacophony of barking. Snarling, they surrounded us as we stood back to back, frantically hitting out with our sticks to keep them at bay. Still more poured in, and more. In bare seconds a whole howling pack surrounded us. For five or six seconds we were immobilized there by a ring of angry animals snapping at us.

Suddenly there was a machine-gun burst of bullets over our heads. A voice called out in German:

"Don't move, throw down what you're holding!"

The soldiers approached cautiously in case one of us might be armed. Then they showed themselves, with machine guns pointed toward us, shouting another order:

"Drop or we'll shoot!"

The jig was up. We let drop our pathetic arms. Immediately, now that we could no longer keep them at bay, the dogs leaped at us with fierce cries. I felt a savage nip in the thigh.

Because the dogs had the taste of blood, the S.S. had trouble bringing them under control. The S.S. themselves were pleasurably excited, rather like hunters elated after a major triumph. To them this was a welcome diversion, a happy romp. Soon more soldiers drifted up, attracted by the barking.

They too were in a skylarking mood. About a dozen of them, and naturally they started to beat us. I got a kick in the belly which bent me double. They cursed, called us *Hurensohn* and *Schweindreck* in the most jovial of tones. Apparently there'd been a bet as to which of the two groups would capture us first.

As far as we were concerned it was all over. A queer sort of dismal relief which I had already felt in the presence of death stole over me. My companions felt the same—resigned and quietly determined not to give way to tears or whimpers before our murderers. They tied our hands behind our backs and kicked us forward.

"March!"

11 UNDER THE GALLOWS

BACK to Auschwitz.

Our hands tied behind our backs, we were set to march toward the prison. And at a hell of a pace too, the motorcycles behind us and the dogs snapping at our heels. They did, though, give us a chance to catch our breath from time to time, as they wanted to bring us back alive. We were dead tired by the time we returned; they had to kick us forward.

We stopped for a moment before the gate. I'd hoped never to see this gate with its terrible inscription again.

A noncom at the gate carefully took down our numbers and then we were led to the Kommandantur to be questioned.

A young elegant officer was in charge and obviously bored with having to waste his time on us. He barely glanced in our direction as he asked if we'd had any accomplices, either within or without the camp. Our brief replies were translated for him by two Polish- and French-speaking Schreibers.

"They say that they have no accomplices."

The blows thundered down on us. As expected. With our hands tied we could not ward off the blows. My share was such that I eventually felt nothing. We were shaken, shouted at, and the questions were repeated more forcefully. But we remained silent and stony-faced.

135

After a while they got tired. Lighting a cigarette, the officer said casually:

"Tell them they're going to be hanged."

And the Schreibers repeated it, barking.

"You are going to be hanged!"

Then we were pushed outside.

"*'Raus!*"

That's all there was of our brief trial.

From there we were led to the Bunker, that is to say the prison. But we weren't locked up in a cell. We were together in an empty room under the surveillance of a Posten. We knew that the sentence would be executed that very night at roll call: no reason to postpone it until tomorrow. Our hands still bound, we wearily slumped down on the floor with our backs against the wall.

Strangely enough, we began to chat, perhaps to avoid having to think. The eldest of the Poles was the first to speak, wiping the blood away from his nose with his shoulder. He spoke slowly in a muffled tone. I tried to make out his words.

"What did he say?"

"He said that we should have left in the afternoon instead of the morning."

And there we were involved in an intermittent discussion, cut by pauses. Perhaps an afternoon departure would have been better after all. Darkness would have fallen sooner and helped to hide us. On the other hand, our pursuers might also have started sooner, so that we'd have been caught right away. Wasn't it rather absurd to be worrying about it now?

A short while later came another sigh.

"We should have waited."

"Why?"

"It seems that the Russians are less than a hundred kilometers away."

True. And a Russian advance might have justified our escape. Who knew that our keepers might not have received an order to massacre us all at the last moment! In any case, why all these regrets when all was lost? Let's get it over with, and as quickly as possible!

The Posten paced back and forth before us, his machine gun slung over his shoulder. Night started to fall. I felt overwhelmed, drained of my last ounce of energy. I only desired desperately to sleep. Let's get it over with, let's get it over with!

A little before six in the evening, we were led to the gallows. These had been erected near the entrance gate, where they could be seen from all the areas where prisoners gathered for roll call. Five gallows, neatly aligned. Five ropes, and beneath these trap doors, worked by a lever. Searchlights blazed up as we approached.

The gallows were at left, facing the entrance gate of the camp. On the right was the bordello. Across what could be called the camp's main street sat the musicians on their platform. This was the hour when work parties came back from their labors. The musicians were tuning up, scarcely casting a glance in our direction. They had the same preoccupied, faintly melancholic air that I had always noticed. Some had probably played there for years. By now the sight of death at Auschwitz had become so common and they'd witnessed so many hangings that five more left them utterly uninterested. Even among the daily total, five was nothing. The musicians on such occasions played, not slow sad funereal music, but a lively and spirited march.

That's the way it was at Auschwitz.

Our S.S. escort fell in on either side of the gallows. The kapos who were to hang us neatly aligned each of us in front of a gallows. Then they tied our feet. After that they brought a stack of signs to hang around our necks, large white cardboard squares on which were written in German: "I tried to escape. No one escapes from Auschwitz. I deserve to die."

To the Germans our execution signified nothing at all, nor did it interest them one way or the other. Making an example of us to terrorize the others who longed for escape was secondary too; to instill the fear of death among condemned men is not exactly necessary. No, what our keepers enjoyed about the ceremony was simply the ceremony itself—an impeccably planned ritual involving a certain amount of grandeur. Like Hitler's mass rallies, an execution at Auschwitz was essentially a public spectacle, and one in which the crowd too played a part. The gigantic pageant must run smoothly without the slightest hitch or false note. From the highest-ranking S.S. to the most abject spectator in his striped uniform, each had to be letter-perfect in his role. Work parties had to be drawn up in perfect order. Musicians had to play just the right tunes with the right cadence. The officer in charge mustn't falter in his speech. Even the condemned men themselves must expire properly.

Otherwise the *Obersturmführer* in charge of the camp would be dissatisfied, and then really important heads would roll!

Sprightly music filled the air. Here was the first work party coming back through the camp gate. Floodlights bathed the courtyard in brilliance.

"*Mützen ab!*"

Marching in columns five abreast, the little group swung into the street, maneuvered on the open area, and stopped in its rightful place beside one of the cell blocks facing the gallows. Ramrod-straight, in beautiful order like crack troops. Their faces remained impassive though they studied us intently. Life being so brief at Auschwitz there were few veterans, few who were really accustomed to the hangings.

Others passed.

"*Links, links!*"

I looked for the faces of friends, knowing there would be some in the second or third work party. Sure enough, before long came two Frenchmen I knew well, walking side by side. As they passed before the gallows they gave me a glazed look of terror that I can see still. That was the only moment that my eyes filled with tears and I had to fight back sobs.

For more than an hour the groups marched by, all at the same regular pace, their clogs slapping the pavement in admirable time with the music. On and on they came until not an inch of space was left. A vast army of twenty-five thousand prisoners, all in their striped uniforms and caps, all at attention. As each work group came up, the kapos methodically went on with their roll call. Only after the last roll call would the army of prisoners have the pleasure of watching the quintuple execution.

The music ended. Dead silence. Then appeared a debonair group of top-ranking S.S., the lords of the camp. Here to lend their presence to the execution, they strolled casually to a spot a few meters from the gallows, chatting among themselves without even deigning to look at us. Beams from the searchlights glinted from their boots.

The officer scheduled to give the speech stepped forth from the group to bark out an address that lasted about three minutes. He listed the crimes for which we were being executed, and then commented on the message written on our cardboard signs, embroidering on the theme that no one could ever possibly escape from Auschwitz and that it was madness to try. Then he rejoined the others, smartly came to attention, and made a crisp gesture for the action to begin.

We doomed men were to be hanged one at a time, from left to right, and I was to be the last: I would be given the treat of watching my comrades die. Two slab-faced kapos came up, roughly seized the first Pole by the shoulders and hoisted him up onto the platform. They strung the rope around his neck and sprung the trap door. Once up on the platform he shouted out:

"Long live Poland, long live freedom!"

It seemed to me that I heard a buzzing rise in the crowd when the Pole called out. And then at the sight of this man struggling on his cord, a merciful curtain fell on my consciousness. I started to live within myself with incredible intensity, my entire mind focused on images of my past life. Even today I can close my eyes and see a vivid picture of that first Pole, spinning and twirling at the end of his rope, his hands tied behind, the huge cardboard sign covering him down to the belly. But of the ones that followed him I remember nothing at all. Perhaps they too cried out "Long live Poland!" I wouldn't know. All that I do recall is the film projected upon my consciousness—fragmentary chaotic pictures from the past and mostly to do with my family. It was the image of my mother who appeared at the very last minute.

And then the rope broke.

Not that I knew it; I didn't realize a thing, having lost consciousness from shock. I didn't even know they had hanged me.

Subsequently I was told that the gaping crowd of prisoners had let forth an enormous "Ah!" when the rope broke under my weight—perhaps because one of the kapos still held on to me when the other activated the trap door. Anyway, it appears that the two men hesitated for a moment, petrified with astonishment, before bending over to loosen the rope from my neck, a coil of which still hung down my back.

As they removed the sign I came to. Or partly came to. It was as if I were in a dream, still unable to realize what was going on around me, aware mainly of the excruciating pain in my neck and back. My mouth was full of blood.

It seems that the kapos called two men from the ranks to take me away. The two men grabbed my shoulders and dragged me off, my feet still tied and dragging on the ground.

Meanwhile, in the ranks of the prisoners, it was being whispered that my life would be spared. In some parts of the world it's an old tradition to grant reprieves to those condemned who survive an execution. And now some of the witnesses to my own execution reported that my reprieve had been granted immediately by the camp commander.

The rumor spread like wildfire through the kapos, despite other conflicting insistence that the officers had said nothing at all. The rumor was born spontaneously in the crowd. No denial came, perhaps to substantiate a belief that German mercy could exist, perhaps through sheer indifference.

Actually, there had never been any question of sparing my life. The S.S. never spared anyone.

Like everyone else I had heard about the little girl, only ten years old, who had miraculously survived the gas chamber —the only case ever recorded by the Sonderkommando. Crushed between several bodies, other cadavers had been piled on top of her in a way that an air pocket had been formed, just enough so that several hours later she was found still conscious amid the mound of corpses. The S.S. did not spare her life. She died the following day, under the needle of a doctor in the experimental section.

When next I became fully conscious I woke up in the Bunker, in the same room where my companions and I had been guarded such a short time before. Confused and helpless, I lay prostrate, moaning, the taste of blood in my mouth. In order for me to get back to reality, someone had to tell me what had happened.

And this someone I suddenly saw before me: the notorious Jacob, chief kapo of the Bunker and the camp's official killer.

I knew him by sight as well as by reputation. A few years before the war he had acted as trainer for the famous boxer Max Schmeling, onetime world heavyweight champion. Interned for many years at Auschwitz as a Jew as well as a communist, Jacob in time had become a kapo. He guarded the prisoners sentenced to solitary confinement and when given the order finished them off with a bullet in the nape of the neck.

A while ago I'd been left there on the ground, like a wounded animal, hands and feet still trussed up, bleeding and barely breathing, my neck throbbing hideously, my head a jumble of turmoil. Untying the rope and lifting me up by the arms, Jacob had half carried me here to a cell. He stretched me out on a pallet and stood frowning down at me—the first sight to greet my eyes.

He was a tall burly man, broadly built, wearing the blue-striped prison uniform with a black Mütze on his head. There were deep wrinkles lining his old boxer's face, which was broad and expressionless. He gazed at me silently. It was I who questioned him in a hoarse whisper:

"What happened? What am I doing here?"

He couldn't manage French, gave a negative headshake.

"*Was ist passiert?*" I translated.

"The rope broke," he replied in German. Using sign language he made me understand that after my fall from the scaffold I had been carried to the Bunker. It took some time for me to grasp all this.

Then death wasn't quite ready for me! Under the gallows, I had impatiently called out for death. But now that a freak of fate had once more seen me through, I began to feel the stirrings of hope, the determination to hold out, to cling to life, to resist.

I lifted my head from the pallet to the man who was already turning away:

"And now what?"

He thrust his hands in his pockets and shrugged his shoulders:

"Now you get a bullet in the head!"

He said this calmly, looking at me out of the corners of his eyes, with neither hostility nor pity. He simply stated that he had received an order to kill me and that he would do so shortly. That's why he was there; he was a camp executioner, given the task of polishing people off with a sort of coup de grâce. All prisoners condemned to death for some lapse or other, when not immediately shot down by an S.S., were hauled to the Bunker and turned over to Jacob. The gallows were reserved for pompous ceremonial executions, mainly for those who had tried to escape. For isolated cases a bullet in the back of the neck sufficed. Jacob had personally rid the world of hundreds of prisoners, whom he stripped of their clothing and then carted off to the crematorium.

He was also the head turnkey; it was he who guarded the pitch-black cells where men in solitary were kept, cramped cells so low-ceilinged and small that it was impossible either to stand or to lie down. Whenever solitary was prolonged for any length of time, the prisoners inevitably died.

Thus Jacob announced that his assignment was to put me

to death immediately without further fanfare. Nevertheless, he added, there would be a slight delay; as he couldn't possibly dispose of all the cadavers until morning, he would allow me to live until then. It was not a question of good will. I understood well enough that he was telling me not to nourish any false hopes. What difference would it make whether he kept a man alive until morning or had a dead body on his hands till then? He would sleep equally well in either case.

I made no response. There was nothing to say: the law is the law. We had been taught obedience at Auschwitz and we had learned our lesson well. Jacob closed the door and locked me in. I heard his footsteps fading away along the corridor.

Semidelirious I lay there groaning, midway between dreaming and sleeping, regaining consciousness from time to time, my mind filled with weird images. Hope would rise one moment, only to languish the next. For such an eternity I had been enmeshed in this immense ruthless machine that ground up men and now I was sick, exhausted, utterly worn out. I wanted only to sleep, and I did succeed in dozing off fitfully every now and then. Each time, though, pain woke me up, blinding spasms tearing through my back at the slightest move.

But gradually I regained some control over my thoughts. Whenever I was able to join two consecutive thoughts, hope again appeared. One fragile fancy, quickly stifled but constantly renewed, kept tugging at my memory. Finally I came to believe there might be something to it, that there might be a chance for me to survive. Jacob was a former boxer. The brotherhood, the interfraternity of sports, might have some effect on him, as it had on the S.S. Perhaps even more than the S.S.

There was a possibility in this that I had no right to ignore. I had a duty not to surrender, not to just give in to the enemy without a fight.

"Jacob!" It came out a mumble at first, then I cried out with all my strength.

"Jacob, Jacob!" I pounded on the door as hard as I could.

What if he refused to hear me out? Or if he only started to abuse me in German, as all the other kapos did when anyone dared to question their decisions. What if he beat me up?

Well, that would be tough. I had made up my mind. With my last vestige of remaining energy I would slam my fist into his face. That way he would kill me on the spot!

Jacob came.

He must have been eating, for he was still chewing and wiping his mouth as he clanked the door behind and put the key back in his pocket. He stared at me coldly.

"Well? What's the matter?"

We stood confronting each other. Once again my fate teetered in the balance, but there was a slim chance. Jacob was a veteran prisoner who enjoyed the trust of the S.S., perhaps even was linked to them through some form of monstrous complicity. So therefore he just might wield considerable power. On the other hand, merely to hide a fairly anonymous prisoner who'd been condemned to death would be difficult enough, let alone a man whose freakish hanging had been witnessed by a crowd of twenty-five thousand. To withdraw one miserable prisoner from a throng of several hundred other miserable prisoners, as had happened in front of the gas chambers, was by comparison a fairly easy matter. After all, my rescuer that time belonged to the master race, so he risked nothing in playing the savior. Jacob, though, was just another prisoner. And a Jew to boot. Wouldn't asking him to save me be the same as asking him to condemn himself? Why should he stick his neck out?

No matter, I had to make my last desperate try, there was no alternative. So I appealed to him, half in German, half in French. I argued that one boxer could not kill another boxer. That he, a former champion, a sparring partner of Schmeling's, could not degrade himself by simply slaughtering me in cold blood. At least I had his attention: he looked at me in surprise.

"Did you box?"

Words poured out of me. I named names, described bouts. And though he obviously hadn't heard of me and my ring career

—he was already in jail at the time of my first amateur bouts—
our common passion for boxing was a bond. I felt that he
was becoming interested, that he was beginning to struggle
with himself. I thought that I detected a flash of something—
was it sympathy?—in his cold gray eyes.

"What's your name?"

"Kessel."

He turned for an instant to glance toward the door and
made a vague gesture. I continued talking, but he wasn't listening any more, he was thinking. And then suddenly he left me.

I was at the mercy of the executioner.

To this day, I haven't a clue as to what happened to Jacob
in the end. During the collapse most of the kapos fled, knowing
they had little chance of escaping the prisoners' murderous
wrath. And in many camps the former prisoners wasted no time
in avenging themselves, so that the bodies of torturers were
found together with the bodies of their last victims. Some kapos
who got away successfully hid themselves, to reappear several
years later under false names; and today they are still alive
leading quiet, law-abiding existences in peaceful German villages. Others not so lucky were taken by the Americans and
Russians to stand trial. Many of these were hanged, for there
was no lack of witnesses to condemn them. A few were pardoned upon proof of having rendered some service; there were
camps where kapos were even involved with the Resistance
groups.

But in Auschwitz, an extermination camp, Resistance was
more or less an impossibility. Here, a kapo's acting as double
agent was unheard of. In any case, Jacob certainly was not one.

The life-giving favor he bestowed upon me was simply the
casual good sportsmanship of one boxer to another, the act of
a man who still felt some link with the past. Far from being a
good man who hated his job, Jacob had never shown the slightest shrinking from the crimes he committed. Without hesitation
he had saved his own skin by agreeing to kill, had become the
Bunker's valued executioner, and performed his services quite

willingly. I am positive that no one before me had ever escaped from his hands alive.

Had he ever been tried, I would have been glad to testify. But what weight could my testimony have carried in the eyes of the law?

For more than an hour, an hour of agonized suspense, I awaited Jacob's return.

He had left me completely at sea as to his intentions. He might easily come back only to shoot me down, feeling he had no choice—after all, why should he risk his own life to save mine? I would have understood that. And as the minutes dragged by, I came numbly to expect it. Any second now I expected him to enter with drawn revolver. The inclination to resist had dwindled away again; I was prepared to drop obediently to my knees for him to put the barrel of his gun against my neck.

So it was another surprise that when he did come back he had no gun, but instead a bundle of clothing. I understood at once.

"Undress!"

Tremblingly I took off my bloody coat, then my pants and my shirt. And then I put on my new uniform. From now on I was to bear another number, written on the coat and on the trouser leg.

"There you are," said Joseph matter of factly. "I'll open the door for you before reveille. You'll have to get out, I can't do any more. Officially I've killed you, taken off your clothes and sent your body to the ovens. On the register you are listed as dead. I don't know you any more, you'll have to get along as best you can."

He spoke without smiling, his tone neutral and without any overtone of friendliness.

Yet he was taking a terrible risk; substituting one person for another cannot be done without danger. Obviously he had a spare body to replace mine, someone whose rags he had given me. In Auschwitz bodies were easy to come by. But if I were recognized, I would surely be put to the question. Perhaps he felt confident that I wouldn't give him away since, after all, I had proved often enough that I could remain silent under torture. How he covered up the fact that someone had been given my number and killed in my place remained a mystery. Perhaps he had an in with higher-ups, or had accomplices below; I have no idea.

At the moment all I knew was that I had to get out of there fast and find some way of blending into the anonymous mass of prisoners.

Just before the siren blew for reveille I went out into the dark night and hugging the walls found the prison block long known to me, which was mainly filled with Poles. I knew that there, in that block, there was a sure hiding place.

12 A CLANDESTINE CONVICT

AND now I succeeded in a deception that only a few months earlier would have been wildly impossible: a change of identity. From mid-December 1944 until the camp was evacuated on the eighth of January 1945, I used a dead man's serial number and got away with it.

Several factors made this possible.

First of all was the extreme instability, the constantly shifting mass of this death camp's population. Daily trainloads of prisoners would arrive and daily the crematoriums and funeral pyres would take their quota of corpses. The kapos, still less the S.S., found it impossible to identify the prisoners who had become mere cogs in an enormous grinding machine. There were so many of these interchangeable anonymous cogs and they were so frequently replaced that the Schreibers in charge could only make a rough estimate in accounting for them. They made many mistakes, giving rise to much irregularity, increased a hundredfold by S.S. thievery. Even the Germans' celebrated talent for organization and administration failed to quell the anarchy and the Schreibers could only cope by juggling the figures.

Secondly, December 1944 was a period of major military upheaval. The Russian advance threatened all the industrial installations in the Auschwitz region as well as those around the other concentration camps. Seeing the handwriting on the wall, the Nazis decided to save whatever possible and to withdraw essential equipment; this made it necessary to change the usual work programs and shift around the teams of workers in order to dismantle the machinery in the armaments factory and load it onto trains. The chill winds of defeat blowing across all Germany had caused administrative chaos.

Also, among the teeming hordes of ill and dying prisoners all wearing the same rags, a person's face no longer had any meaning and could no longer serve as a means of identification. Gaunt, hairless, wearing the same grisly mask of pain and terror, each skeletal head resembled another. Of an evening when the prisoners were allowed to wander from one barracks to another, I could mix with any group at random without being spotted as a newcomer.

During the next weeks I couldn't avoid running into two or three acquaintances who recognized me. But they thought that I had been reprieved. That rumor which had made the rounds on the day of my supposed execution still hadn't been scotched by the authorities. Nor did I confide the truth to anyone.

In any case, my fellow convicts had neither the time nor the inclination to dwell on such trivia. It was all they could do to stay alive themselves. For at that point, famine was in the land, and our already inadequate rations were halved. We were half crazed with hunger.

Just the same I took precautions. The first most obvious thing was to move away from my old cell block and to avoid my former work groups. Even more vital, I mustn't be glimpsed by any of the kapos who knew me. Somehow I must become part of a new environment yet remain unnoticed, relying on the vast upheavals and turnovers to preserve my anonymity.

Finding a sanctuary didn't take long. I wasn't a veteran of Auschwitz for nothing! Under the roof of the barracks where I used to sleep—which was now occupied by Poles—there was a tiny sort of false attic. It was easy enough to climb up there; the difficult part was to stay still once you got there. I had to stretch out on the floor and not move a muscle as long as a living soul downstairs was awake. But once they'd gone to sleep I could slither down from my perch, look over the free space available and quietly slide under a blanket to sleep beside some unknown convict.

Eating was a far worse problem. The first couple of days I managed to steal some bread by scouring the deserted dormitory. The Poles living there had the privilege of receiving parcels. But the crumbs I could glean from these wouldn't have kept a bird alive. I reluctantly concluded that my only recourse was to go back into the ranks and get a worker's share of the food.

First I merged with a gang working on the railroad. But I only stayed there three days, the work being so rugged I figured it would kill me quicker than malnutrition.

Consequently, I managed to join a team working on the water distribution system. That was better! All I had to do was carry loads which bent me double. What really helped was that for some mysterious reason the kapo in charge liked me. Why this man, who was intrinsically just as brutal as the others, should be kindly disposed toward me I have no idea. Just one of those things. He was a German who'd worked in Luxembourg before the war and spoke a little French as a result. After a few days he appointed me to do odd jobs: cleaning the barracks, chopping wood for stoves, etc.

These extra bits of work on top of my regular job brought me an extra ration of soup, which I was able to trade for bread. Food was more plentiful than ever before during my last few weeks at Auschwitz, and, just as important, there were no beatings. This precious respite allowed my back to heal and me to store up vitally needed strength for the last struggles to survive. Although the Germans were being inexorably pushed to the wall—and we could see more and more evidence of their coming defeat—they nonetheless were determined to get on with their project of mass extermination. Freight cars full of human cattle still pulled in at the Auschwitz platform, and the smokestacks of the crematorium belched black clouds until the very last day.

Meanwhile we could hear the Red Army's cannons in the distance.

Now I was bound and determined to stay alive. Paradoxically, my long experience as a convict helped me to do so. Here at the end, we veterans escaped the blows that rained down on the newcomers. Newcomers always suffered the most at Auschwitz. Fearful, unadjusted, disorientated, and disorganized, they knew nothing and dared nothing. They were always getting into trouble from not knowing the ropes. Their greenness sheltered us veterans. That is the hard law of all prison systems.

I knew how to hide when danger lurked and to reappear when it had passed. I could gauge to the split second when the sentinel would turn his head, I knew when and how to slip unobtrusively into a group, how to find the safest hiding place.

All in all, during those last days of the camp's existence, I was able to make the most of the ever increasing disorder and inevitable slackness in discipline. The camp's command structure began to waver, from the top brass all the way down to the work teams.

In this hectic period I lived in a perpetual state of driving anxiety. Every uniform that appeared at roll call made my heart beat like a drum. I knew that at any second I might be forced to reply to some question, and then the jig would be up. I could hardly sleep nights.

All that upheld me, as it upheld all the others, was the growing certainty that soon, soon, Germany would be defeated. Just to live until that happy day became everyone's consuming desire. Every air raid made us jump with joy. The first time we could distinctly hear the cannon, one January morning, while we were marching through the snow, an excited murmur went through the crowd, caution thrown to the winds.

Then we heard that the Red Army had freed Russia and

invaded Poland, and we knew that our masters must tremble in their shiny boots.

One day an S.S. motorcyclist screeched to a halt near the site where we were working. It was a little after noon, in the brief pause following the distribution of our soup. It was January 18, 1945.

The S.S. man approached our group. I thought for a moment he had come for me. An absurd idea; how could he have time for anyone so insignificant in the storm that was overwhelming Germany? He beckoned the kapo to one side and gave him some terse orders. Then he jumped back onto his motorcycle and roared off. I gathered from this that he was speeding from one work site to another leaving the same instructions.

Immediately we were marched back to the camp. Within a half hour a milling mass of prisoners filled all the free spaces between the barracks. All the work parties had assembled. We waited expectantly for the usual interminable roll call to begin. But there was no roll call. We were amazed. An assembly without a roll call of prisoners was quite inconceivable.

"Everyone to his barracks!"

What happened next seemed even more astounding. Men were sent to the kitchens for soup and returned bearing treasures such as we had never laid eyes on in the camp: whole loaves of fresh bread, cans of corned beef, and sticks of margarine. Hardly able to believe our good luck, we feverishly divided the food among ourselves, each of us getting quite a lot. The kapos warned us that we had better make it last, but we weren't having any of that! Wolfishly we tore into the feast.

We wondered what could be happening. So did the kapos. They only knew what their orders said: to bring us back to camp, lock us up in our barracks, and bring us food. With the first edge off our appetites we started to invent stories. Most of the prisoners thought that our keepers would eventually flee and we'd just be left to our own devices. They believed that the approach of the Red Army had impelled the Nazis to empty their storehouses of food, which otherwise would be wasted. And indeed the Red Army's progress, according to all the reports that reached us, did seem rapid enough to justify such a hypothesis. Others of us thought we would be mobilized to build defense works behind the lines.

Meanwhile the kapos and Blockältesters had left us alone. We saw them crossing camp headed for the main offices, and they were gone for over an hour.

When they came back from the conference they told us what had been decided.

"Auschwitz is going to be evacuated. Every man must pick up his personal effects, his blanket, and the food he's been allotted. Assemble for departure at eight o'clock this evening."

We felt more confused than ever. We couldn't believe that the whole camp would actually be evacuated in a body. Why, there were tens of thousands of us. Even those who could accept the idea of a massive departure could consider only a short march in stages, to another part of the Auschwitz compound. No, said the kapos, the whole outfit was being moved, we were all retreating to another camp in Germany. But they didn't tell us in which direction.

In point of fact, they didn't know. We dared question them and were flabbergasted at their civil responses. Here were the torturers discussing things with their victims!

These men who had showered us with many a blow now didn't even show us their clubs. They didn't insult us. There wasn't an ounce of menace left in them. They allowed us to question them and even deigned to answer. There was fear in their eyes. They were afraid of falling into the hands of the rapidly approaching enemy and having to answer for their crimes. And they were afraid of losing their power in this vast upheaval, of suddenly becoming disarmed and vulnerable to reprisals from the prisoners. What if they were ousted from the camps? Here they were kings, but banished from their little kingdom they risked an awful descent into nothingness.

All the judgment we had left told us the entire moving operation was insane. How could so many people be moved, and why? Now that Germany had lost all hope of victory, what possible good could be accomplished in keeping this multitude of slaves? Whatever work they were still capable of couldn't stave off defeat. Quite the contrary, such massive movements would be expensive. We would require an armed escort, we would block all the highways, fill up space on the trains, and create bedlam in all the camps to be submerged by this tidal wave of refugees.

If the idea was to have us die on the journey, we reasoned, it would have been much simpler to exterminate us right then and there, rather than stretch out the massacre over thousands of miles. The roads would be littered with corpses.

And if they hoped to conceal from the world what Auschwitz had been, well that made no sense either. Never could they wipe out all the evidence that it had existed—that was quite impossible.

We were baffled. We still assumed that our nighttime departure in the freezing cold would be postponed, that a counter-order must inevitably come.

But no! The weird operation was going through, and that was that! Logic didn't exist in a defeated Germany led by a madman. We were going to be thrown onto the roads.

13 EXODUS

On this January 8, 1945, there was no way for me to predict that my life as a convict would last another five months. Five months during which a fanatical Germany would blindly continue to fight. Meanwhile, as the troops retreated, camps were evacuated.

Auschwitz with its various dependencies contained almost two hundred thousand prisoners. Not all of these could be allowed onto the open road at the same time. The Germans couldn't run the risk of a massive revolt. On such a scale as that, they would never be able to put it down. With all of us together, we couldn't help but realize our strength and exert it to free ourselves.

So we were split up. Our various departures were staggered over several days, and each group took off for a different destination: Ravensbruck, Oranienburg, Buchenwald, Mauthausen, Dachau; almost every camp in Germany received its quota of prisoners from Auschwitz and the annexed compounds.

At the same time the concentration camps in the west, which felt pushed by the advancing Allied armies, also sent their inmates toward the center. In general, the prisoners moved in his way had to undergo the ordeal of several such hikes.

157

Barely had they arrived weary and travel-worn than they had to drag themselves off on another exodus.

I only had two such killing journeys to make: from Auschwitz to Mauthausen and from Mauthausen to Gusen II. On both, conditions were so atrocious that half the men in my group died along the way. And the same was true in many other groups. Thousands and thousands of dead bodies were strewn along the highways of a conquered Germany.

Naturally, the mere two hundred thousand prisoners evacuated from Auschwitz represented only a small percentage of all who had entered the gates since its establishment. All the rest —the large majority—went to the crematoriums. Auschwitz crematoriums had reduced several million people to ashes.

Out of these two hundred thousand survivors, fewer than half lived to get home. And of this number, only about two or three thousand were Frenchmen.

Right away the Germans solved the problem of how to evacuate sick prisoners, many of whom were terminal cases: they abandoned them without food. When the Russians reached the camp a week or so later they freed those who still lived, as well as the handful of nonpatients who'd taken the grave risk of remaining behind in hiding. Though the S.S. ferreted out and killed most of those who tried to hide in the barracks, they didn't find them all, even with their dogs. In such a hasty departure it was impossible to examine every nook and cranny.

I too had planned to hide, since I knew better than most how to go about it. But there was no time. All at once we were surrounded by menacing soldiers and told to move fast! We were as always mortally terrified of the S.S. These shouted, as they brandished their arms, that they would tolerate no relaxation in discipline, on pain of loosing their dogs on us, and we believed them. We had no notion of resisting. The temperature was well below zero.

Resisting! We trembling ragged men clutching our few provisions to our scrawny chests had no resistance left in us. Crushed by the past and overwhelmed by our present danger, we could think of how best to hold out, and to hope that it would be our neighbor rather than ourselves who fell under the inevitable bullets, blows, and illness.

We started our march already miserable, exhausted, cold, and hungry, not a normal healthy man among us, but still in our ranks of five abreast.

There were nonetheless a few successful escapes along the way, just as there had been desertions during our departure. Those who made it were mainly Poles who knew the region and thus could rely on some help.

The grapevine had it that the Germans would blow up Auschwitz before they left. In the end they only partially destroyed the crematoriums.

However, they did burn the archives at the very last minute. On leaving, we could see bonfires blazing in front of the barracks. Orders from above had been to eradicate every possible trace of the S.S.'s crimes. They did a good job, considering everything.

But it's not for lack of evidence that twenty-five years later the trials of the S.S. are still continuing, or that some have never even been brought to trial. Many of them stayed happily at home all these years without even having to answer a question or seek refuge abroad.

The trip from Auschwitz to Mauthausen lasted thirteen days. For a week we marched in the snow twenty or thirty miles a day, across southern Poland and Czechoslovakia. The rest of the trip we made by rail. All we had to eat was the food that had been distributed before our departure. All we had to protect us from the biting cold, besides our threadbare uniforms, was a thin tattered blanket.

The wooden clogs under our bare feet didn't offer much protection against the frozen ground we walked on. Anyone who stumbled from exhaustion hadn't a prayer unless he was helped by his neighbors. And only rarely was he helped. Usually, an S.S. would drag him by his heels from the column into a ditch and put a bullet through his head. All up and down the line we could hear the crack of firing. A man near me who couldn't keep up the pace was shot down still standing, on the flimsy pretext that he was trying to escape.

In this mad exodus all organizational structure vanished. Ties formed in barracks or in work teams no longer existed in this struggling mass of humanity stretched over several miles. Those marching around me were virtually all complete strangers, and in extremis one doesn't bother to get acquainted. When we were given a rest break, we could only sink down and try to regain a little strength, each man cut off from the others both by choice and by necessity.

When, sometimes late at night, we reached a farmhouse where we could take shelter for a few hours, it was invariably too small to house everyone. So the last arrivals would have to spend the rest of the night in the snow. And naturally by the time morning came a lot of them were frozen stiff. Others still alive lay there motionless, supine, unable to get up. These the S.S. would finish off with their revolvers.

Back on the road again, we could hear the revolvers spewing death behind us. And the farm was always searched afterward, the S.S. using their trusty dogs to find the hidden men.

On the third or fourth night I had the bad luck to be one of the outdoor sleepers, it being impossible to squeeze into any of the buildings where we stopped. Every barn, every stable, was crammed with bodies, stacked up as if they were so much kindling wood. I shiveringly stretched in the snow with the others, having no choice, and with chattering teeth rolled myself in my miserable little blanket. It is very easy to sleep in the snow and I slept soundly. The next morning, the whistle for reveille brought me from a lovely dream in which I saw myself free again.

I felt lightheaded, yet heavy of limb. With infinite trouble, I got up on my feet, found myself once again in the ranks being pushed forward by the crowd. I found it hard to breathe, or even to see clearly. Suddenly I collapsed. My two neighbors leaned over me, saying that I was feverish and they would help me. And so they did; they supported me, almost carrying me at times. Had it not been for these two selfless men, my body would surely have frozen there on the Polish highway. Later I tried to find them to express my thanks, but I was never able to do so.

When I could once again walk without help, I took a handful of snow from beside the road to quench my thirst. This made me feel a little better and I was able to make it to the end of the day's march.

At the beginning we'd been buoyed along by the hope that we would be unable to keep ahead of the Red Army's lightning advance. We dreamed about the Red Army. It was the sustaining dream in all our imaginings and, when we had the strength, in all our talk. Every distant rumble of a bombardment rekindled new hopes. But the Russians were never able to catch up with us.

We advanced slowly along the road, stiff-legged and mechanical, our torn clothing increasingly muddy, our hands and feet half frozen. Sometimes we met civilians along the road. They would stand with averted eyes to let the marching ghosts go past. As we approached villages we could see the inhabitants fleeing in terror of the incessant shots accompanying us.

One evening we drew up to a switching yard. After the torture of the road, we were to be subjected to that of the train. I thought I already knew the horrors of being shipped and could not have believed that this was to be even worse. After beating us aboard with rifle butts they forced us into open freight cars meant to transport equipment. They were small cars and normally would hold about twenty men. But the soldiers packed seventy of us aboard.

Had they allowed it, we could have crowded aboard in parallel lines, each man seated between another's legs. An uncomfortable position, but in this way we could have managed without being crushed. But no, the S.S. didn't want to see any heads rising above the edge of the flatcar. The point, naturally, was to prevent escapes. They felt there were too few of them to cope with us.

And so we were forced to lie down, one on top of the other, all tangled and mixed together. Each car was like a flat dish packed to the brim with stacks of interlocking bodies. Not a hair showed above the edge. The S.S. guaranteed this by firing machine guns over our heads. Only when the crowd of prisoners was quite flattened out did the train start.

For five days we lay there almost motionless and without so much as a crust, or a drop of water. Even when the train would stop for hours at a time, shunted off on a parking track, we were not allowed to stir. The S.S. didn't want to bother running after anyone who tried to flee, much less escort people who needed to visit the latrines. They preferred to have a train-load of corpses, and would silence a cry quite simply with a bullet.

In the terrible cold many of the inert bodies slowly gave up what remained of life in them. When the train began to roll, the rush of freezing air would chill us to the marrow. It did not look as if there would be any survivors by the time we got to Mauthausen. Later someone told me he had witnessed a poor lunatic gnawing at the flesh of a dead man.

On the afternoon of the second day, in a station whose name I still don't know, the train stopped for several hours, somewhere in Czechoslovakia. This time the S.S. allowed us to sit up, so we got the chance to stretch our frozen legs. Thus some of the townsfolk saw us, shivering in the open car with our blankets over our heads. Our ghostlike faces aroused their pity, and some of them decided to help us.

There was a sort of footbridge crossing the rails as far as our car. The kind Czechs came along this footbridge carrying loaves of bread, cheese, and cakes, and tossed them to us. And, horribly, we tussled each other for the food, baring our teeth and snarling. Of course all prisoners in all camps had fought for food, but it seemed somehow more degrading in these close quarters, surrounded by the dead. Even the weakest would strike out feebly in an attempt to grab bread from another's mouth.

Suddenly we heard rifle shots. The S.S., alerted by the noise we were making, came up at a run. They didn't even take the trouble to order the Good Samaritans to go away. They simply fired on them point blank. Screaming, the Czechs took to flight and all got away except one. He lay on the footbridge, a pool of blood streaming from beneath his riddled body.

I spent the last two days in an on-again-off-again coma. Noticing that my two nearest neighbors were dead, I took their blankets and then snuggled under their stiff bodies for warmth. Occasionally rousing to consciousness, I would hear the death rattles of those around me.

On the evening of the fifth day we reached Mauthausen. We were ordered to get off the freight car, and I was strong enough to get down. In the few moments we waited on the platform, I tried to count the men who had survived and could still walk. There were nine of us from our car. And the pitiful groups clambering off the other cars were no larger. There were still living men among the dead aboard the rolling coffins, but they were unable to get up. I don't know if they were shot or left alone to die a more lingering death.

14 MAUTHAUSEN

WHISTLES, assembly, rushing hither and yon. Dozens of police dogs growling at us. Even in our moribund condition we still had to form columns *zu fünft*, and march in step. The Nazis had really proved that the limits of human endurance can be pushed to an indefinite point. That even dying men could be made to troop in unison.

"*Vorwärts, Marsch!*"

In our filthy rags, we marched ahead stiff as boards but in ranks. We didn't feel the cold, our once aching bodies had become numb. Lined up as in our best days at Auschwitz, we marched the three miles to the camp.

"*Links, links!*"

The road climbed up toward a camp we could see at a distance in the midst of a desolate landscape. From what we had heard the Danube wasn't far away. Soon we saw the prison walls. Then once more we were inside prison and we knew that Mauthausen was a punishment camp, *Nacht und Nebel*, from rumors we had heard.

For those of us waiting with bated breath, this was a terrible disappointment. We would have to hold out a lot longer. We tried to console ourselves with the thought that if the Russians didn't reach us perhaps the Americans would and

165

they were richer and perhaps had kindlier thoughts as far as we were concerned. In any case, we would be repatriated quicker, we told ourselves—Mauthausen is in Austria not far from Germany's southern frontier. As far as we could judge on the basis of the news we had received early in January, the conquering Allied forces had pushed into Germany some time ago. So it wouldn't be long before they reached us, barring some near-miracle that would give the Wehrmacht new life. We knew for sure that the invaders were crushing everything before them. Surely we could hold out for a little while!

The minute we arrived at camp, we could see smoke from the crematorium chimneys polluting the night air, and we could smell the familiar sickly sweet odor. Well, nothing had changed in that respect! And as we went through the gate, we had to execute the *Mützen ab* and *Mützen auf,* and here again were a bunch of mean-looking kapos ready to take over. We prisoners who had eluded death on the trip now had to start fencing with it all over again. But first we had to get through the night.

No shelter was available to receive us. All the barracks were packed with prisoners, many of whom like us had come from the outside to await orders. We learned that we'd be sent to one of the other annexed camps around Mauthausen. Meanwhile, as there was no space indoors, we would sleep out in the open air.

Luckily it wasn't quite so cold as it had been my last night in the snow. And at least we wouldn't have to lie on top of each other. We slept on the frozen ground of a courtyard between the kitchen building and the crematorium. Once again we huddled close to one another for warmth. A smell of rotten cabbage emanating from the kitchen mingled with the stench of the nearby latrines and served to distract our nostrils from that worst of all odors—the ovens burning the dead.

They hadn't fed us, of course. This was normal, since we weren't registered for the moment. Until the Schreibers wrote our names down in their books we weren't officially part of Mauthausen's population and technically didn't exist. Paperwork would be done in the morning.

At sunrise we were taken to the showers. And here were the devilish kapos again, so remarkably like all the other kapos we had known. Instinctively we bent our backs and assumed a defensive posture, our frightened eyes watching for the movements of their rubber truncheons. Crushed into shower stalls too small for even half of us, we crowded under the spigots from which emerged a trickle of hot water and tried to finish quickly to placate our screaming guards. We weren't much cleaner when we came out, but anyhow we had warmed up a bit for the shaving ordeal.

It was still tedious, and humiliating, to have to spread our thighs. The specialist shaving me tried to chat, perhaps because he felt lighthearted about the prospect of being free soon, and he made a crude pleasantry on his status of ass-shaver. No one, he boasted, could do the job quite so quickly or as thoroughly. I'll have to admit that I was in no mood for jest. Never had I felt so weak, and never had my body seemed so pitiful.

Then the kapos rushed us to the quarantine barracks, with us running naked as usual pursued by our pack of demons. They put us in a wooden barracks similar to the one I had known at Birkenau; apparently only the *Wäscherei*, or showers, had been built of bricks. Once in this abode we were supplied relatively clean rags. There was no question of our having beds. Since men in quarantine do not work, they obviously have no bed priority and must sleep on the floor.

We were fed, though, and this enabled me to make another comparison. The soup doled out at Mauthausen tasted even viler than Auschwitz soup; in fact it literally stank. Nevertheless we gobbled it down greedily as we'd had nothing warm in our aching bellies for over two weeks. Here in the barracks, which we couldn't leave except to go to the latrines (and then only with permission) we began to indulge in the luxury of talking.

We had revived somewhat from last night, and we told each other what we had heard by chance here and there. Other prisoners who had arrived before us had been able to get a little information. It appears that at Auschwitz a few of our kapos had been found dead under beds or hidden elsewhere. Just to think, while we were sleeping outdoors, several of our Auschwitz tormentors had been killed! Apparently the S.S. couldn't have cared less and made no pretense at finding the killers. We thought it might have been some of their fellows who murdered them. Room could not be made for the Auschwitz kapos without displacing the Mauthausen incumbents. And the local team had obviously fought back, with, doubtless, the tacit agreement of the local commanders. It seemed that still another aspect of contention existed in our little world of dog eat dog. In every camp the "political detainees" always clashed with the "common law criminals." And it appeared that by the time we got to Mauthausen a group of politically oriented kapos had succeeded in establishing, their authority. I never got to the bottom of this story, not wanting to squander any of my precious store of energy to do so.

Certainly we had no reason to mourn the passing of our former kapos—though we saw soon enough that our new ones weren't any more humane than the old ones. They employed the same rubber weapons, which they used as often. We had the same cringing necessity to cower beneath their hail of blows. Mauthausen was no different from anywhere else.

However, for a while life was easier because of our quarantine. We were in a special section where we need not work, and we determined to make the most of our holiday, to the extent that this word still had a meaning. Despite our isolation, we veterans managed to swing a little extra bread thanks to discreet deals with the kitchen staff. I got some of my strength back and the pain in my spine diminished.

Pretty soon we began to suffer from a sort of population explosion. Men were streaming in from all over Western Europe, most of them in frightful physical condition.

Our masters could no longer handle this mob as efficiently as formerly. They resorted to sending droves of the sick prisoners to the infirmary, where they died like flies.

Confined to our quarters, I saw next to nothing of Mauthausen. We were deluged with macabre stories of torture before the wailing wall and on a gigantic staircase which led to the quarries. But what could a description of one hell mean to us who had just come from another?

One morning the yelling kapos rushed in and kicked us out of our quarters. 'Raus! Outside. And that was the end of our lovely quiet. Once again we paraded before the Schreibers, those capable and conscientious bureaucrats who always wanted to know our names, ages, and professions for their endless forms. Nowadays they were a little hampered by the sudden overcrowding, of course, but they still continued to operate just as they had in the past, true to their customary methods. The amazing part was that the Schreibers seemed under no illusions about their country's coming defeat. Yet they never flagged; as the Third Reich shrank inexorably under double thrusts from the east and west, the Schreibers were still prodigiously filling out reams of forms in every corner of Germany that hadn't been invaded. All the administrative machinery continued to turn like clockwork although the Americans were only a few miles away, and cities were aflame on all sides.

Our new serial numbers weren't tattooed on our forearms of our quarters. 'Raus! Outside. And that was the end of our wrists. I received number 118900. No one noticed that my initial serial number was the one of a man who had been hanged. Dead men disappear quickly. Only two months had passed and Sim Kessel was nothing but a memory. Still I was careful, though it may not have been necessary, to give the Schreiber working on my form a false name.

So there I was, a brand-new person, and that gave me a certain amount of relief. The guilty, unpunished prisoner of Auschwitz, who had once escaped from camp, from the gallows and from the crematorium, ceased to exist legally. I became only an innocent prisoner bearing a regulation serial number. A serial number is everything; it dispenses you from having had a name, having had a soul, or having had a life.

After our midday soup, we learned that we were to be sent

to another camp, an annex of Mauthausen. It was impossible to remain in the central camp, stuffed as it was by an incessant flow of incoming refugees. The quarantine section had to be cleared quickly.

And so we were sent to Gusen II.

15 GUSEN II

ONLY a few miles west of Mauthausen, the camp of Gusen II bore a sinister reputation even among concentration camps. People died there more quickly, it was said, because of the crushing work that was involved in building a factory for Messerschmidt under a mountain. For some time now German industry had been digging underground to escape the bombardments. Here was certainly proof of Germany's being on its last legs, not having enough planes to defend its factories; but for us who worked there it was terrible. Not that pick-and-shovel men have ever enjoyed a very easy life.

Though not of the same imposing size as the main camp, Gusen II was just as strictly guarded. Barbed wire and watchtowers. And of course there were both the S.S. and the kapos. Barracks were dilapidated and stinking and too small for us. We saw at once that we had to sleep three in a bed, but we were accustomed to that. Anyway, a black sagging mattress stiff with dirt and half filled with broken straw is an element of comfort not to be disdained even if you can occupy only a third of it. You can certainly rest better there than you can on a bare floor.

Our serial numbers were recorded by the Blockschreiber, and we went through all the other formalities.

Next, as in all the other camps, we were given a lecture by a formidable Lagerältester assisted by interpreters. He was a corpulent, red-faced man obviously accustomed to strong drink. He paraded before us waving a huge *Gummi* for emphasis as he spoke. I can remember most of what he said, and while the text hardly differed from what we'd heard many times before, the venomous delivery was rather special.

"You are now at Gusen II—a concentration camp, not a rest home."

That part at least was pretty familiar, as was his reference to the Himmelkommando, the sky commando where we'd all be sent after we had finished at the crematorium.

"You must be clean here. There is nothing with which to wash. We have neither soap nor water to wash with nor time to wash, but we are still clean. And if you are not clean, you die. Is that understood?"

We had to reply *Ja!* in unison.

"Here you obey orders. The kapos know what you must do. If you are ordered to carry a stone weighing a ton, you will carry a stone weighing a ton, and if you are ordered to eat shit, you will eat shit. If you refuse to obey you will die. Is that clear?"

"*Ja!*"

"Here there is somebody who will teach you how to obey, and that's me! You don't know me yet, but you will get to know me. I've killed thousands of men like you. I like to kill. When I kill I enjoy it."

That this was no mere blustering I had plenty of opportunity to learn later, watching this assassin and his henchmen murder indiscriminately as if they were swatting flies. Their superiors the top brass, far from restraining them, offered every encouragement. Next morning, as part of a work team collecting corpses, I began to get an idea of what life was like at Gusen II.

During the first few days, before assigning us to groups, they gave us odd jobs cleaning up the camp. A few others and I were ordered to get rid of the bodies, the most unsightly and unhygienic form of garbage. In the infirmary and in the dormitories, corpses were stacked up (higher piles in winter) and left a while so as to save on transportation. The barracks chiefs derived some profit from this, acquiring the prisoners rations by postponing the notice of their death.

Pushing our barrows we would go to every barracks to be told which stacks of bodies to pick up. Corpses were generally laid out on beds—naked, ice-cold, and stinking. The infirmary kapo in charge of the operation kicked us as he gave the orders: two of us would grab the dead man's shoulders and legs and then run to dump him into our barrow. Action must be double time. While we raced with our body, a third man standing in the cart would neatly stack the cadavers up like cordwood, one atop the other, to make as much room as possible.

I can still hear the hollow sound of their skulls cracking against the slats of the car and the kapo's harsh voice swearing at us in the filthy words that seemed to constitute their vocabulary. Still running, my teammates and I would push the loaded carts to the crematorium, there to unload the carcasses one by one, piling them up along the wall to make tidy stacks.

Handling corpses was nothing new to me. In Auschwitz I'd often had the same job. But the corpses at Gusen II sickened me. Matchstick legs and arms, cancerous skin, and infected scabs from which pus still flowed. Several bodies were still befouled from the dysentery that had killed them. Contact with this putrefying flesh made my teammates and me retch. Our pus-covered hands filled us with horror. We thought the stench of death would never leave our clothing.

Our gruesome job lasted a week. Then we were healthy enough to perform more strenuous work. Despite the abundance of manpower Gusen II managed to consume workers at a fantastic rate. Each day the teams would return with their quota of ill and wounded to be taken to the infirmary. Soon it became our turn to labor at the underground factory.

One morning at five o'clock sharp we were marched some distance from the camp to be loaded onto a train, to the usual concert of shouts and blows. The cattle cars had to be boarded in measured seconds, and when we arrived at our destination in the Danube Valley they had to be emptied just as fast. Germans always insisted that their trains or trucks be emptied and filled on the double. Woe be unto those who were clumsy or lagged behind.

The ride lasted only half an hour. As we got out of our cars, they were instantly filled by the night shift workers. Black with grime, the workers leaped aboard to return to camp. Work at the factory went on around the clock.

On that first day we were assembled in front of shops and divided into work groups according to our capabilities. Each shop needed skilled workers. A Schreiber read out a long list of skills and withdrew from the ranks those who claimed to be qualified. It seemed all too clear to me that unskilled workers would be sent straight down to the subterranean infernoes of quarries and galleries. The unskilled had to fill the gaps caused by the deaths of former unskilled workers—until they too died there. Gusen II veterans had said that four or five weeks was about all you could hold out for inside that mountain, breathing dust for twelve consecutive hours as you wielded a pick and shovel. Then when you couldn't stand up any longer they would haul you back to the infirmary to die.

In other words it seemed vital to try to sneak into one of the shops. So I said I was a sheet metal worker. My name was duly recorded and two or three of us were directed to the sheet metal section.

Of course I hadn't a clue as to what sheet metal was all about, or for that matter what any industrial skill was all about. I could just as well have claimed to be a lathe operator, an electrician, or a fitter. But when I saw that the Schreiber was nearing the end of the list I nervously declared that I was a sheet metal expert without waiting any longer to hear a more familiar-sounding trade. Of course exposure would mean being thrown out of the shop and sent to join the common laborers *after* being beaten for my trouble. But that would be just too bad! I had to take the risk. Daring, I have often noticed, pays better dividends than caution.

And so it proved on this occasion. I happened to get a civilian supervisor who appeared to be quite a tolerant fellow. He was an Austrian, a man who knew his craft and how to manage a team of workers. After asking me a few leading questions he readily understood that I was a rank imposter who'd never held a mallet in my life. He simply shrugged, went to fetch a wooden form, put a piece of sheet metal on it, and showed me how it could be shaped with the mallet. Patiently he watched my first clumsy efforts and then took the tool in hand himself to correct my mistakes.

At first I thought my Austrian Meister had a heart. Actually, he was afraid. From time to time, when he was sure there were no S.S. around, he would open up and speak his mind. *Hitler kaput,* he said. Most of the time he was quite pleasant, didn't shout or harangue us. Knowing how near the Americans were and that they would soon be invading the region, he didn't want to be denounced as a man who mistreated prisoners.

So ten of us spent our working hours in relative comfort, spared any physical injuries and hardly even seeing the murderous kapos. Fine. But once we left the shop to go back to camp we were vulnerable again, at the mercy of kapos on the ride and later during the interminable roll calls. Every other week we did the night shift, which naturally meant we wouldn't get much sleep.

Weeks passed. More and more often we could hear the air raid sirens. One day the Meister mentioned that the nearby town where his family lived had just fallen into enemy hands. I could hardly conceal my elation and couldn't resist the impulse to pass the word to my French comrades working in another tunnel. I asked permission to visit the latrine and on the way ran to tell my friends. They'd already heard, having read the news in a local paper their shop foreman had left behind.

Alas, in my exuberance I hadn't noticed an S.S. man following me into the shop. Nor was I aware that he was now hiding behind a machine and watching me confer happily with my friends. The machinery's clack-clack and the bustle of the factory had lulled me into a false sense of security. Suddenly the S.S. bounded forth to yank my jacket with a force that nearly lifted me off the ground.

What was I doing there! he thundered. I had to confess that I really worked at another shop. That did it. He kicked me every step of the way there. Then he ordered me to lie down on the work bench and to count out the regulation twenty-five strikes as delivered them *auf Arsch.*

I started to count: *eins, zwei, drei,* while he struck savagely with his whip. This was the third time that I'd had to suffer this form of torture. From experience I knew the first blows were the worst and I determined not to give him the satisfaction of hearing me scream. Amazingly, he stopped when I got to *einundzwanzig,* saying that he would spare me the last four blows because I had not cried out.

My hind quarters felt as though the skin had burst open.

Rising painfully to hoist my bloody trousers, I again took up my mallet with a trembling hand. My disciplinarian gave me a few clouts on the head for good measure, cursed roundly, and promised to send me to the quarries next time I gave any trouble. Then he turned to the Meister who'd been watching pale with fear for his own safety. Any more lax discipline in the shop, he said, and the Meister would get a black mark too. Majestically he strode off, striking his glistening boots smartly with his whip.

That punishment provided the same aftereffects as always —I could neither sit down nor stand up. Though the skin wasn't broken, my whole body hurt and I could barely walk. For the return trip I could only get back into the freight car with the aid of friends. And of course I didn't sleep a wink that night.

But the next day's events more than wiped out all my aches and pains. Reveille sounded, but not roll call! The Blockältester came to inform us curtly that we would not be going to work that day and to stay put. He gave no further explanations.

Naturally we were all agog, alternately imagining the best and the worst. Not knowing what to do with ourselves, we wandered around the barracks. We were too intimidated to dare go out for news. One idea that had occurred to us when we were feeling discouraged was that the S.S. would choose to massacre us rather than allow us to be freed by the invaders. Occasionally we seemed to hear some machine gun bursts in the distance as if to confirm that thought. But now my comrades came running up in a dither to say that the S.S. had disappeared!

Everyone immediately rushed outside, and sure enough, there wasn't a single S.S. in sight. Only some old soldiers of the Wehrmacht, mostly old men who appeared to be the dreg ends of the reserve, stood guard. There were plenty of them, and the machine guns in the watchtowers were still pointed at us, but the S.S. had disappeared! And the night shift returning from the factory confirmed the good news that the S.S. couldn't be seen anywhere!

Our excitement kept mounting as the day passed. We didn't work, or do chores, or even have roll calls. All sorts of rumors floated around. Some of the prisoners, who still expected a massacre, tried to organize a plan of defense against it, but nobody paid them the slightest attention. Any sort of calm discussion was impossible in our agitated state. We all seemed to have lost our senses. For what really thrilled us, what drove us to transports of delight, was the thought not of freedom but of food. To eat real food again! That was all we thought of.

Today we were still given the same slop as before. From that standpoint at least, nothing had changed. The soup detail went to the kitchen and came back with the same ordinary rations.

On the other hand, a miraculous improvement could be seen in the kapos' behavior. It was the same metamorphosis I'd seen at Auschwitz. The kapos suddenly stopped bellowing and began to confer softly among themselves. They gazed inattentively at us wrangling over bread without wading in to whale the daylights out of us. For now they were actively concerned about their own getaway. They were preparing to flee.

Actually we could have attacked them, and they'd have gone down like ninepins from the sheer force of our numbers. And the old relics who were guarding us from the other side of the barbed wire probably wouldn't have intervened. But we knew nothing for sure, and could only wonder and wait impatiently.

That night there was some pillaging, and many accounts were settled. But we knew nothing of this. Lying on our vile mattresses in filth and sweat, we didn't realize that this would be our last night as prisoners.

Next morning I was wakened by the sound of other people waking, rather than by the customary whistling and shout of *Aufstehen!* When I hurried outside the barracks I saw that there were no longer any sentinels, no longer any soldiers in the watchtowers. And no more kapos! Our incredulous eyes opened onto a silent, abnormal, incomprehensible world without masters and without rules. A vacuum. We stood there, turning our shaven heads to look wonderingly at one another, our eyes blinking in the light of a beautiful May morning, as we cautiously advanced step by step.

We saw nobody around but us nobodies. Aside from us there was only the vermin we slept with, that was all, just the fleas. The jackbooted autocrats and their vicious kapo attendants had gone. These terrible despots, who made the earth tremble with their presence, who ordered us when to work and when to rest, who distributed bread and pain, who had power over life and death—these lords had at last disappeared.

16 LIBERATION

I CAN remember almost every moment of May 7, 1945. It was my first day of freedom. Though I still wore the striped uniform, I was no longer a slave. Barbed wire still surrounded the camp but the guards had gone. Like the rest of my comrades I was intoxicated with joy, yet confused and unable to make plans; apprehensive of what might lay outside yet chafing with impatience to leave.

No one remained to imprison us, there were no more machine guns on the watchtowers and the gates were flung wide open, but to us, Gusen II was in limbo, nowhere. Our group consisted mainly of Poles and Russians, plus a few Spaniards. The French were rare.

For us to leave the camp would be to take on the mysterious unknown. We had neither guides, nor maps, nor weapons. No one could either control or lead this motley turbulent mob.

Suddenly freed of our jailers and thrown into a state of anarchy, we didn't even have sense enough to elect chiefs. For all we knew, staying in the camp represented still another risk —we had no idea what might be going on on the outside. The fear that our guards might return and punish us somewhat poisoned our jubilation. We had no way of knowing that this was impossible.

Even if we had known, we would have been unable to really grasp the fact and believe it. Shut up like animals in a cage for months or years, brutalized by hunger and misery, thirst and fear, we were delirious, wild. No one who has not gone through it could possibly understand our mixed emotions. Every camp had become an insane asylum.

All our normal reflexes as civilized men had been destroyed, obliterated along with our individual personalities, and replaced by mere primitive instincts; we suffered from that terrible neurosis acquired in concentration camps which to this day many of us have never been able to shake off. In this sordid hole at the end of the world, surrounded by a virtual wasteland, we were fenced in by barbed wire which we believed to be electrified. So we remained isolated and withdrawn, with no other rule of behavior than our previous one—preserving our own skin.

On that first day, our primary and most driving urge arose from our starvation. Seeing that the warehouses and kitchens were no longer guarded, and that not a single kapo could be seen anywhere, we made a universal rush to the available food.

In a basement corner I came across a sack of potatoes and madly gathered up a couple of pounds. A fellow prisoner, a Belgian from Brussels, joined me and helped carry my booty. He was to become my last friend in prison. What the others found I didn't know or care—I paid no attention to them, considering my potatoes a precious treasure.

The Belgian and I found an out-of-the-way spot where we could cook and eat them, still afraid someone might come along and grab our prize away. In great excitement we broke up an old bedstead, started a fire, and began to roast our potatoes. But we couldn't wait for them to get done, we wolfed them down almost raw, and never has any food seemed so delicious.

As we heard the sound of doors being battered outside we hid the rest of the sack and went out in search of more loot: i.e., food. Everywhere we looked we saw stealthy groups of men doing the same—looking warily around for a private place where they could eat.

It must have been about ten o'clock when the sound of an engine made us rush to the barbed wire. An armored car was advancing slowly along the edge of the camp and the American star insignia could be distinguished on its side. The vehicle stopped about twenty yards away, its guns pointed straight at us.

Within seconds there were several hundred of us prisoners there, shouting and yelling at the apparition in every known language, but not one of us thoroughly institutionalized men dared venture beyond the barbed wire. The armored car stayed there motionless and unresponsive for five or six minutes, and then the motor started up and our silent visitors backed away.

Though hopes of our immediate liberation had vanished, we were nonetheless able to look to the future with more confidence. At last I had seen the armed and helmeted soldiers of the conquering army; I had seen them with my own eyes. We could no longer doubt their presence. And we could reasonably assume that they occupied the entire region.

Nevertheless we were still bound to the camp. We had only seen a reconnaissance outfit. Perhaps the victory had not yet been complete, and the invaders were busy crushing the German resistance. That certainly took priority over coming to the rescue of a few thousand prisoners. In our total ignorance, we dreamed up and believed all sorts of speculations, and I didn't fail to exchange my share of gossip and guesses with the other inmates, however absurd they might prove.

Pandemonium reigned. Fifteen hundred half-crazed men milled about the open prison they dared not abandon. Sheds were overturned and given to pillage and thousands of hated objects thrown out.

First the *Schreibstube*, the hall where records were kept, was devastated. In our eyes the most pressing goal was to dig out, divide, and hoard away large quantities of food. We didn't know that Germany had already surrendered, we didn't know anything. All around us lay terminally sick prisoners incapable of getting up, whom we didn't even think of helping. To relieve these dying men in any way never even occurred to us. There were also corpses which had not yet been taken away; they continued to rot untouched.

All we could think of doing was to pillage, and even in this activity we kept the suspicion and pusillanimity of slaves.

Midway during the afternoon we discovered two kapos hiding in one of the sheds. Apparently they had mistakenly decided not to flee with the others the night before.

Perhaps they'd hoped to anonymously mix with the crowd of prisoners when the Americans arrived, to remain unmasked in the chaos of liberation and eventually have themselves sent home to Germany as victims of the Nazi terror.

They obviously hadn't considered that the Americans might wait before occupying Gusen II and that the restless idle prisoners would roam the camp and rifle it from top to bottom.

The two men were dragged from the shed, and at that moment their shrill cries attracted my attention. Grabbed by the arms and legs and around the neck by a gang of frail prisoners drunk with fury, the brawny kapos trembled and begged for mercy, trying to ward off the blows that rained down upon them.

Their clothes were ripped off their bodies. They were robust and hefty, and obviously capable of defending themselves against the feeble crew of skeletons who were attacking them. They did not, however, offer any resistance at all, seemingly paralyzed by fear, and only attempted to shield their heads with their elbows.

As they squealed their tormentors kept striking, awkwardly bumping into one another in their frantic haste, kicking the kapos and slamming bony fists into the loathed faces.

The circle of spectators screamed, their faces distorted with hate, like madmen. The two victims disappeared in the center of the frenzied group leaping haphazardly about. Soon they were to be seen again. Stretched out on the ground, entirely naked, their faces swollen and covered with blood, they shrieked unceasingly at the top of their lungs.

Fiercest of all were the Russian prisoners, who shoved and pushed each other out of the way so as to get nearer their victims and to boot them savagely, again and again, in the crotch.

Soon long iron bars were found on a stack of building materials and triumphantly brought forward. The circle spread out around the two flailing bodies and the iron bars went into action. They were slung in great arcs, bouncing against one another with a hideous clang, crushing the torsos of the two unfortunate kapos, making the blood spurt. The men twisted for a long time under the blows and then stopped moving.

This was the last murder that I witnessed. My failure to play a part in it, I must admit, was not due to any humane scruples but simply to my physical debilitation . . . I just hadn't the strength to wield a heavy iron bar and force myself into the circle of prisoners. If I had been stronger, I'm afraid that I would have willingly participated in the grisly deed.

Horribly mutilated and bathed in blood, the two corpses were dragged by their feet into a cell block and left there.

Toward dawn on the eighth of May, the same armored car we had seen the day before reappeared, but instead of entering the camp drove eastward. A few minutes later, a second showed up and continued along the same path. News of this had been brought to us by our comrades stationed at the barbed wire. At this word, Charles and I decided to leave camp—Charles being my new-found friend of the night before.

Barely older than I, he too had been arrested for his underground activities, deported to Oranienburg and then evacuated to Mauthausen. Though he had suffered much less than I, having been caught much later, his desire to see his native land was as imperative as my own. Even the night before he had proposed that we take off in the dark toward the Allied lines. He believed, and rightly, that we would be repatriated most quickly if we took the first step instead of hanging about in endless lines of prisoners forming in the camps for eventual departure.

I agreed, but felt that leaving during the night was pretty risky. We didn't know but what there might be some S.S. hidden in the neighborhood. Alone and unarmed, ignorant of routes, we might pass within range of their guns and they could pick us off like sitting ducks. Better to wait until daylight, when we could at least see the terrain.

Finally I convinced him. So at about seven o'clock in the morning, after packing up a little food, we sneaked out along the deserted road, in the direction from which the armored cars had come. Soon we saw a signpost indicating that Linz was fifteen miles away—the obvious direction to take, for this Austrian city must surely be already in the hands of the Americans.

Hope supported us all that day, for we were hardly able to walk, much less undertake such a hike. But we staggered on, covering the fifteen miles during the afternoon, and finally limped into the city at dusk. Wonder of wonders! We were agog at a world we couldn't have believed existed—civilians calmly walking about, children playing on the sidewalks, shopkeepers standing in their doorways.

Occasionally through an open window we could glimpse a cozy interior. It seemed incredible that there could still be an orderly universe where couples could live happily together, sleep under sheets, sit in comfortable armchairs, rock babies in cradles. Inconceivable that anyone could freely stroll about on his own instead of marching in step or cringing from an expected blow.

The city, at least the part that we saw, had not suffered from the bombing. We had no trouble locating the Americans, they were everywhere, helmeted, in battle dress, bristling with their fantastic equipment. We approached them confidently, sure that our prisoners' rags would win their instant concern and good will, that they would welcome us with open arms, help us and repatriate us. What an illusion!

No one paid us the slightest notice, and the strapping soldiers that we addressed indicated briefly that they couldn't understand us. We could not speak their language, and they had other business at hand. We could understand the indifference of the Austrian civilians, brainwashed as they'd been by propaganda and warned against us—particularly as they themselves were dying from malnutrition and openly begged from the conquerors. But the Allied troops! Didn't they care?

We had no idea that droves of other deportees had flocked to Linz after escaping from neighboring camps, and that their sheer numbers had almost overwhelmed those whose business it was to take them in.

In any case, we could never tire of gazing at the splendid robust soldiers whose existence had made us free. Casual and strong, these happy warriors strode into the cafes laughing and joking, tossing candy to the little Austrians. Clean, bursting with health, impeccably uniformed. Their huge, shiny, brand-new machines were parked bumper to bumper in the streets; their trucks carried mountains of foodstuffs.

And we derelicts, weaker and hungrier by the minute, wandered through the town, vainly trying to make contact with these huge well-fed youths who couldn't understand us, who'd had no orders concerning such as we, and seemed to regard us with more mistrust than pity.

Somehow, all of us concentration camp alumni had assumed that a fate as cruel as ours was bound to be known, that the monstrous conditions in the concentration camps would have aroused the indignation of the entire world. It came as quite a shock to realize that this was not true, that people knew nothing at all of our plight, and that to these soldiers we might just as well have been criminals who had escaped from their prison.

Suddenly we became shatteringly aware that we meant exactly nothing to anyone.

At last, however, we found an American noncom who spoke German. He seemed moved by our story. He went away and returned with two packages which he presented and then departed again, slapping each of us on the back. The packages contained cookies, chocolate, and cigarettes.

We ravenously devoured the food at a gulp, then luxuriantly smoked, marveling at this inconceivable windfall. Unfortunately, our debilitated bodies couldn't take it. Within an hour we had terrible bellyaches. Night was falling. Full of self-pity, we began to wonder what would become of us, whether or not we would have to collapse there on the cold wet pavement.

Just then, though, the sight of a French uniform gave us new hope. Here was a soldier drastically different in appearance from the American troops. His filthy uniform was in tatters, his puttees torn. It developed that near Linz there was a French prisoner-of-war camp from which he had just been released.

Young, rather thin, smiling and friendly, he understood what we were talking about. He had already seen men from the concentration camps, though we were the first who spoke his language. He took us to his camp. And there we learned that the Americans were concentrating the deportees at the Magdalena camp, where the prisoners of war were being held.

Our new friend introduced us to his buddies, who cordially received us, celebrating our arrival by pressing on us all sorts of delectable goodies such as bread, bacon, sugar. They couldn't think of enough ways to show their kindness and commiseration. These men, who had suffered for five years, understood that we had suffered even more than they. They thronged around to hug us. How long it had been since we had basked in such warmth! So long, in fact, that we had trouble believing it wasn't a dream and finally, when we did believe, we broke down and bawled like babies.

Beds were produced for us, not bunk beds stacked one on top of another, but proper beds with springs and woolen mattresses, perhaps looted from a neighboring house that had been gutted by a bomb. Once their guards disappeared, these war prisoners had done their utmost to make their quarters comfortable.

Now we benefited from their efforts, but couldn't get used

to our sudden well-being—this unwonted cleanliness, the queer softness of the mattresses under our bruised, lacerated backs, and above all by this boundless space which allowed us to stretch out our arms and legs all we wanted.

Alas, I could not enjoy the luxury, for I was very sick indeed. My friend Charles, more fit than I, seemed able to keep down the bacon that he had eaten. All night long I was racked by hideous dysentery, an affliction I'd suffered aplenty at Auschwitz, but never like this; I had to get up more than fifty times during that single sleepless night. By morning, there was little left of me, wasted as I was by the illness on top of my general debilitation.

The French soldier who brought me my breakfast cup of coffee was alarmed by my appearance. He immediately ran off to fetch the two camp doctors, who were also prisoners of war. They tapped and poked me and then they examined my emaciated carcass that still bore the marks of its last beating.

After a quick exchange of looks the two doctors soothingly tried to reassure me with the verdict that there was nothing much wrong, certainly nothing that called for drugs (fortunately, as they had none anyway!). They recommended that I drink plenty of water and refrain from overindulging in bacon —the remains of which lay in an unsightly mess beside my bed. Above all, I was to get lots of rest.

There was certainly no argument there! I wanted to say that I'd have little trouble obeying their orders—the mere thought of bacon and/or getting up was revolting—but I couldn't even summon the energy to speak.

As they withdrew, I saw the physician nearest the door give a kind of sad little shrug in answer to Charles, who was questioning him. In the doctor's mind there must have been small chance of my making it, for the whole scene smacked of deathbed drama, a "make his last days happy" aspect. They said I'd be as right as rain after a little nourishment—soon I'd be back in Paris.

They brought me milk to drink—the Americans had flooded

the camp with their powdered milk—and my friends lavishly displayed their concern with offerings of fruit and candies. I thought I was going to die there, like an idiot, only a few hours by plane away from home, after having lived through the rest of the hideous ordeal.

The very thought made me angry. I decided that if I was going to die, I was going to die at home, in France, and not here.

Will power must be behind every strong act, and once again it enabled me to pull through. Not without grueling exertion, however. Never, never, had I felt so tired, so spent and limp. Even during the darkest days at Jaworzno and Auschwitz, when my physical condition made me ripe for the ovens, I wasn't on the verge of expiring as I now was. I needed every ounce of my friends' moral support to make the required effort. They knew that I needed them and they didn't let me down; they came in relays to my bedside, around the clock.

One day they told me that I was due to go with the others to Magdalena, where all the rest were being held in quarantine. The American doctors, it appeared, were afraid of epidemics, and had no intention of repatriating sick or contagious men. They planned to cure them first, and obviously, they could take far better care of me there than I was receiving here.

By any standards of logic I should gratefully have sped there. But I vehemently refused, I absolutely would not go into quarantine. Come hell or high water I determined to get to Paris as quickly as was humanly possible, whatever the consequences. Even if it meant dying upon my arrival there.

Since soldiers had been given priority over the deportees, I resolved to stay with them.

One of the two doctors that came to check on me each morning patiently tried to reason away my foolish obstinacy. He said that he himself would take me to the quarantine camp and wield his influence to get me the finest medical treatment.

But I was adamant. The mere idea of being with a mob of ex-prisoners made me shudder. I wouldn't go, they couldn't make me go. The kindly doctor must have thought that I had lost my wits. He insisted no further.

And yet though my cause was indefensible, in the long run it would be successful—not, needless to say, by due processing through all the channels, but by deceit.

French soldiers are fairly crafty by nature. These good men brought me a rather worn private's uniform and a cap. They also produced a pair of boots from somewhere. And not only for me but for Charles, as we had decided to stick together. Then they pointed out the barracks where orders were cut and where the records were kept.

Sim Kessel laboriously arose, dressed himself with the aid of his comrades, and joined the ranks in the line waiting for repatriation.

An overworked noncom took his name down as a soldier in an infantry regiment and a prisoner in stalag. His civilian address was enough. Without further ado he received an official, multistamped document assigning him to an American transport plane which was to take off the day after next from a nearby airport.

The trick had worked, but I nearly passed out from sheer suspense before getting back to bed.

Two days later we all set off in the morning. They couldn't get a car for us and we had to hike to the airport some ten miles away, but who cared! All my pals were there to lend good cheer as well as occasional physical aid. At times when I had to stop and go down into the ditch, for I was far from cured, they waited patiently for me.

Toward the end of the march, however, fear of missing the plane forced them to hurry. They had to continue on without me, calling back encouragement for me to join them. It was nip and tuck in my condition. I got to the airport, in extremis, half an hour after the others, but still before takeoff. I showed my official paper, the only kind of identity I had on me, and at the last second was shoved aboard an enormous aircraft, where my friends greeted me joyfully. The rapture of actually getting away at last erased every memory of my ordeal—all I could think of was my homecoming.

An uneventful trip. Four hours' flying time. The plane put us down in Rheims and a truck carried us into town to a park. Here we were to be picked up by another military vehicle the next day.

Only I didn't have the patience to wait there with the others. To mark time for twenty-four more hours was quite impossible —I thought I might die before then. Without saying a word of farewell, I callously slipped away from my friends and ran to the station. While in prison I had acquired the habit of sneaking off from groups and the thought that this was an unfriendly act barely touched me.

In the crowded station there was another little wait for the right train, but finally one pulled in. A train crammed with people, yet I managed to stretch out on the floor of the corridor.

The nearer we got to home, the more I began to worry— for days now a thought had been trying to insinuate itself into my mind: what about my parents? Were they still living? In three years, anything could have happened; they might have been sent to the gas chambers. Naturally there'd been no means of getting news of them while I was a prisoner. And I hadn't attempted to write from Linz, for not only was I too feeble to hold a pen, but I was put off by the fear that my letter might come back marked "address unknown."

Stretched out on the gangway of the train, I counted the minutes. Once at the station, in Paris, I hoped to find a taxi and go straight away to the Place Daumesnil, where my parents lived.

But it was not to be. Descending to the quai I was greeted by an unexpected hubbub and fanfare. It seemed that a welcoming service—most unwelcome to me—had been arranged for the returning soliders, with pretty hostesses serving refreshments while officers issued orders.

They told me to get in line with the others for entertainment. I didn't dare protest or refuse, despite my itching desire to skip it. Dominated by the age-old prisoner's fear of punishment, I meekly filed into line. The trucks bore us away.

They took us to the Gaumont Theater, which had been requisitioned and made festive to receive the ex-prisoners of war. Speeches, sandwiches, candy; and part of the treat was a Laurel and Hardy film. I was glad it wasn't dancing!

I tottered to my seat and dropped off to sleep the moment the comedians flashed on the screen, waking only when the lights came on again.

Lovely girls were passing along the aisles dispensing fruit. One of them stopped abruptly before me, her eyes wide with shock.

"Good heavens, what stalag were you in?"

In fact, I must have looked like a cadaver. The rest of the boys had their own pressing problems to worry about and hadn't noticed that there was a wraith among them. Only this perceptive girl with her basket of fruit noticed. She had seen thin prisoners before, but this was something else!

At first I hesitated but she insisted on an answer.

"I wasn't in a stalag at all," I admitted.

"Where then?"

"I was at Auschwitz."

She remained speechless for a moment and then rushed to tell the authorities. At once a lieutenant with a staff of two nurses arrived, questioned me, said I wasn't well enough to be at the theater and that I must go to the Hotel Lutetia where all the deportees were being taken care of.

Suddenly I found myself being whisked into an ambulance which had been ordered especially for me. And with a nurse in charge. It looked as if the reunion with my parents was going to be delayed a while longer.

At the Hotel Lutetia another officer queried me at length and in detail about life in the concentration camp—which of my arms had been tattooed, and so on. It seems they had to be very careful in order to rule out imposters, but once convinced of my genuineness they installed me in one of the Lutetia's most luxurious rooms.

Here they dosed me with medicine and promised that from now on I would receive the very best of care. The only trouble was I didn't want it.

Still fearful of any kind of authority and not yet readapted to human kindness, I received this benevolence with the same hostile resentment with which I had endured cruelty. It would take me some time to regain the outlook and responses of a normal human being. I was suspicious, ungrateful, unsociable, antagonistic, reluctant to ask for anything or even to speak. And yet I felt this immense longing to see my parents, an urge that surmounted all other emotions.

My last escape was child's play. Early the next morning I simply tiptoed from my hotel room and left the premises, amazed by the easy success of my audacity.

At a nearby cafe I tremblingly telephoned the head of my old network. Why hadn't I thought of that sooner? His wife answered, surprised and happy to recognize my voice. My parents? Yes, they were alive and well . . .

Later I learned that the Resistance had come to their aid, supported and protected them, providing all the false documents they needed to escape the Nazis. The Resistance really was a marvelous outfit.

A few hours later, I was finally able to rejoin my family in their temporary home at Villeparisis. And then my true rehabilitation began, for without them, I would never have recovered my enjoyment of life.